CHINA SINCE MAO

Neil G. Burton
Charles Bettelheim

Monthly Review Press
New York and London

Copyright © 1978 by Monthly Review Press
All Rights Reserved

Library of Congress Cataloguing in Publication Data
Bettelheim, Charles
  China since Mao
    1. China—Politics and government—1976- —
Addresses, essays, lectures. I. Burton, Neil G.,
joint author. II. Title.
DS779.26.B87   320.9'51'05   78-15623
ISBN 0-85345-474-4 cloth
ISBN 0-85345-475-2 paper

Monthly Review Press
62 West 14th Street, New York, N.Y. 10011
47 Red Lion Street, London WCIR 4PF

Manufactured in the United States of America

10 9 8 7 6 5 4 3 2 1

CONTENTS

INTRODUCTION
by the Editors

On May 11, Charles Bettelheim submitted his resignation as president of the Franco-Chinese Friendship Association, citing growing misgivings about events in China since the death of Mao Tse-tung and disagreements with the attitude of the dominant faction within the association toward the post-Mao Chinese leadership and its political line. Professor Bettelheim's letter of resignation was published in somewhat abbreviated form by *Le Monde,* and through this and other channels reached a wide international audience interested in developments in the Peoples Republic.

Several months later, in October 1977, Neil Burton, a Canadian living and working in Peking, addressed an open letter to Professor Bettelheim in response to his letter of resignation from the Friendship Association. Mr. Burton sent copies of his open letter to Professor Bettelheim and to the editors of MONTHLY REVIEW, together with a covering letter in which he suggested that MR should publish the original letter of resignation, his (Burton's) reply, and whatever rejoinder Bettelheim might care to make. Following this suggestion, we asked Professor Bettelheim, whose book *Cultural Revolution and Industrial Organization in China* had been published by Monthly Review Press in 1974, whether he would be interested in participating in such an undertaking. He replied that he would but that the pressure of other work would prevent his doing so for some months. This explains why a project initiated nearly a year ago is only now coming to fruition.

Concerning his text, which was finished on March 21, Professor Bettelheim wrote in his introduction to the French edi-

7

tion: "As the reader will see, my letter to Neil Burton, rather than being a simple response, is a first effort at systematic reflection on the political changes which have taken place in China since October 1976 and on the conditions which prepared the way for them."

The Editors

LETTER OF RESIGNATION
to the Franco-Chinese Friendship Association
by Charles Bettelheim

May 11, 1977

Dear Friends,

As you know, the events which have followed the death of Chairman Mao have deeply worried me. Like many other friends of China, I have felt serious apprehensions for the future of socialism in China since the arrest of the four leaders who played a central role in the course of the Cultural Revolution and who—with the exception of Chiang Ching—enjoyed the confidence of Mao Tse-tung.

The charge that the Four tried to carry out a coup d'état is in no way convincing. It is general practice for people who have successfully carried out a coup to claim that those they have deposed were trying to seize power by force.

My doubts with regard to the political consequences of these events are all the more serious since two of the arrested leaders, Yao Wen-yuan and Chang Chun-chiao, have made an important—even though incomplete—contribution to the analysis of the class basis of capitalist restoration in China.

However, whatever my worries and doubts, it seemed to me indispensable, before taking a position, to see what arguments were advanced by those who have taken over the leadership of the Chinese Communist Party, and what actual political line was going to be followed by them. What has transpired in the course of the more than six months which have gone by since the events of October 1976 unfortunately have only confirmed my fears.

The way in which the "criticism" of the Four has been and is being conducted has nothing in common with Chairman Mao's teachings. There is no Marxist analysis to be found in the published material, simply slander and scandal, the low level indicating the inability of the present Chinese Communist Party leadership to develop any serious criticism of what the Four's political line might have been.

During the campaign conducted against the Four, one finds accusations which apply directly to the practices of the current leadership. One can read that the "falsification" of photos to which the Four resorted proves that they were at once both "vile conspirators and opportunists wanting to seize the party and the state" (Hsinhua dispatch; March 27/77). Condemning the falsification of photographs and every distortion of historical truth is certainly just; however, these practices presently predominate, as can be seen, for example, in the double issue of *China Reconstructs* of Nov.-Dec./1976, where falsified photographs appeared openly.

Other accusations made against the Four negate the very requirements of Marxism. Thus, for example, the reproach made against Chang Chun-chiao for having wanted to carry out a class analysis of present Chinese society and, furthermore, of having wanted to develop Marxism—this is called a denial of scientific socialism and counter-revolutionary revisionism.

Other accusations are still more unbelievable or, if they were to be accepted, would raise serious questions as to the lifestyle of the leading cadres of the Communist Party—such as the accusation laid against the Four of having meals served to them in restaurants without wanting to pay for them; of that addressed to Chiang Ching of having ordered an "Empress' dress."

Finally, other accusations amount to exaggerations which openly misrepresent the facts; they are gross falsifications. Thus, newspapers and magazines of the last few months have said that the Four lived a decadent and corrupt bourgeois life. Wang Hung-wen is said to be a typical representative of the new bourgeoisie. The Four are said to have obstinately upheld the positions of the landlords and the bourgeoisie, and to have been 100 percent committed to the capitalist road. They are presented as sworn enemies of the Communist Party, of the working class, of the whole people and the Chinese nation; as being guilty of espionage, of capitulating to foreigners, of importing instruments intended for the use of their secret agents, and of importing luxury articles. They are stated to have deliberately squandered state funds in order to damage socialist accumulation, and to have exalted material incentives. They are even presented as Kuomintang agents.

If such accusations correspond to reality, that could only cast the gravest doubts on the composition of the party leadership and on Mao's own vigilance. If they were true, we might well expect some or all of the present leaders also to be revealed in due course as Kuomintang agents guilty of "spying for the enemy."

But if, as I believe, the charges do not correspond to reality, it is impossible to trust leaders who deceive the people by eliminating those with whom they have disagreements, not by clearly explaining the basis of the disagreements, but rather by resort to slanderous attack.

Under these conditions, one is inevitably led to the conclusion that the fidelity to Mao Tse-tung's political line is simply a smokescreen designed to conceal a quite different line. In fact, an examination of texts published in China during the last few months, as well as what it is possible to establish as to actual practice, has led me to believe that a revisionist line is presently triumphing. The criticism of Teng has been abandoned, while calls giving production primacy over revolution predominate. Discipline and order are exalted, while there is no longer any question of the right of people to reserve their opinions, not to mention the right and duty to rebel against a bourgeois policy. Questions as to the position of women during the socialist transition period are denied. The struggle against bourgeois right is scarcely mentioned anymore. The problem of the existence of the bourgeoisie within the party is juggled away. An appeal to class struggle is replaced by an appeal to struggle against the Four.

In an all-around way, the necessary criticism of the Four is conducted from a revisionist standpoint and not from a revolutionary one. No distinction is made between what they might have said or done wrong, and the points on which they might have been correct. More precisely, their mistakes are used in order to reject their correct analyses as well, in contradiction to the requirements of dialectical materialism, and in a way that reinforces bourgeois ideas.

What we know of what is going on in China confirms the revisionist orientation of the present policy. Factory regulations are becoming oppressive. Open-door schooling has practically been abandoned. This means that while paying lip-service to the Cultural Revolution, its gains are in the process of being liquidated.

As far as foreign policy is concerned, the struggle against the two superpowers has gradually been replaced by a struggle against social-imperialism alone. As a consequence, United States imperialism is denounced less and less. Its interventions, or those of its allies, in the life of other peoples, are frequently even seen as "positive" — this was the case with the events in Zaire. But when two imperialist bandits are confronting one another, it is wrong to take the side of one against the other. The present international practices of the Chinese Communist Party damage China's prestige with people, especially in the Third World. In fact, these policies play into the hands of social-imperialism.

Such is the judgment which I am driven to make on what is happening at present in China. We have too little information at our disposal to know the magnitude of the forces opposed to the present political course. Certainly these forces exist, as testified to by the scale of repressive actions of the last few months. It is impossible to predict under what conditions and over what stretch of time China will get back on the revolutionary road.

Experience shows us how much the present leadership of the Chinese Communist Party uses every sign of approval from abroad to try and increase its prestige with the Chinese masses. Thus to give approval to the political line presently dominant in China, or even to maintain an attitude that might appear to be approval, is of service neither to the Chinese people nor to all those who are struggling for socialism in China.

The Franco-Chinese Friendship Association is dominated by a trend which supports the present Chinese Communist Party leadership—this in spite of doubt felt by numerous friends of China within the association. From that I draw the conclusion that it is correct for me to present my resignation as chairman of the Franco-Chinese Friendship Association, which is what I am doing through this letter. I request that you please transmit this to the National Bureau and to members of the association, and present the text in *Aujourd 'hui la Chine.*

I extend to you the expression of my friendship and solidarity with the Chinese people.

Charles Bettelheim

IN DEFENSE
OF THE NEW REGIME
by Neil G. Burton

October 1, 1977

Dear M. Bettelheim,

Earlier this year I was much disturbed to hear that you had resigned the chairmanship of the Franco-Chinese Friendship Association. Since I had read and learned much from several of your works (*On the Transition to Socialism*, with Paul Sweezy; *Cultural Revolution and Industrial Organization in China; Class Struggles in the USSR*, Vol. I), I was particularly anxious to know what factors and what analysis had led you to conclude that a "revisionist line" was now triumphing here in China. Last week I finally had the opportunity to read the full text of your letter of resignation.

As I went through your letter, I was struck by how many of the points you made were the very points that have caused me much trouble over the past year — and how many of them have likewise been raised by other worried friends of China. And yet, when I had finished reading I couldn't help feeling that your analysis was less than adequate, that your case that a revisionist line predominates was far from being a solid one. How could this be? How could an eminent Marxist intellectual who had delved so deeply into the specific problems of revisionism and capitalist restoration be so wide of the mark?

I've reread your letter several times and turned it over in my mind, and I'd like to set forth a number of items for your consideration. I won't try to answer each of your doubts in detail: partly because the necessary supporting documentation would

15

be voluminous; partly because I still agree with several of your points myself; and partly because I believe that most of your doubts stem from a very few questionable practical and theoretical assumptions. Since I believe these assumptions to be widespread outside of China, I wish to tackle them at some length. I also wish to treat this as an open letter so that others may participate in the clarification of the issues I raise.

Firstly, I believe that you have jumped too fast. All of us who have more than a passing interest in China, like the vast majority of the Chinese people, were uncertain what would follow the death of Chairman Mao Tse-tung. Those of us who are friends of China or supporters of socialism were apprehensive about the possibility of reversals, or revisionism. I believe that, unlike many Chinese, the majority of us foreign friends of China — and particularly those who attempt to understand China within a Marxist analytical framework — were rather inadequately prepared for events as they actually transpired. Of course we shared the view with most Chinese that the reversals could only come from the Right. But what most of us failed to understand, or at least failed to grasp in a practical way, was that the Right is so discredited now in China that it can hardly present itself in other than a Left guise. But even if we did grasp this, the limitations on our sources of information left us much more poorly prepared than many Chinese for what happened. Those of us whose forte is theory were very sure that we at least knew who the real "revolutionaries" were, so our attention was focused on the others, those leaders whom some have called the "pragmatists," others the "bureaucrats," but in any case, the ones whose intellect hadn't caught our attention in print. The most dangerous of the rightists had already been taken care of through the campaign against Teng Hsiao-ping and his "Right deviationist wind," or so it would seem from the sources — printed sources — available to us. So our worries were somewhat abated when the anticipated, but still numbing, news of Chairman Mao's death reached us. The key point here is that, even if the spectacular "reversals" of last October caught us off guard, we nevertheless already had fashioned logical categories within which to fit them.

Your letter suggests that your immediate response to the news of the downfall of the Four was negative. But as a man of some considerable experience, you hesitated to be too rash; you took a wait-and-see attitude. Consider my position here. I, like you, wanted very much to see socialism built and consolidated in China. I, like you, am trying to use Marxism as a tool to understand — and hopefully to change — the world. Unlike you, I was in China, working as a "foreign expert." Yet still, like you, I had no privileged sources of information, nothing that could have prepared me for the October events ahead of time. My logical categories (even after three years here) were, I suspect, not much different from yours, since my interests, if not my experience, seem to coincide in large measure with your own. Thus my immediate reaction was probably rather similar to that which struck you. But there was a complicating factor. Unlike you, I was employed by the Chinese government. How long, after all, does one go on working for a cause that one believes to have gone wrong?

What was it that allowed me to stay on? Simple opportunism? I prefer to think not. Rather it was the almost immediate realization that something was wrong with my logical categories and the subsequent revelation that I had been misled by the very propaganda — printed propaganda — from which I had been deriving the bulk of my knowledge about the political events going on around me. And how did I determine what the flaws in my logical categories were and begin the process of rectifying them? To be frank, it didn't come about without much confusion, pain, and soul-searching.

I was in Shanghai when the first official word of the arrest of the Four came, in conjunction with huge street demonstrations held to celebrate their fall. That was two weeks after the arrest itself, about ten days after I had heard the news on the Voice of America, and one week after I had seen my first posters against the Four in a railway station in Pengpu City in eastern China. The first question I had to confront was why such huge numbers of people were able to participate with seemingly great enthusiasm in celebrating what I saw as a "reversal" — and in Shanghai, the very city that had been the Four's home

base. The demonstrations were organized, of course (to an out-
sider it seems that virtually everything is organized in China).
But joy is hard to simulate, as the earlier demonstrations concerning Teng's removal had proved to those equipped to see.
Was it all just another part of a meaningless ritual arranged to
legitimize a top-level power play, as some Western analysts
would have us believe? Or were there really so many domestic
enemies of socialism just waiting for the downfall of those I saw
as its major champions? Were Marxists living in a theoretical
dream-world while most of the people were really for capitalism after all? Had Chairman Mao been wrong when he said we
must place our faith in the masses, rely on them? I couldn't
answer any of these questions satisfactorily at the time, but I
certainly had to admit that the logical system I had been relying on was inadequate.

A few days later I was back in Peking with family, friends,
and colleagues. People I knew and who knew me. Though my
Chinese colleagues exhibited varying degrees of enthusiasm,
for the most part they, too, seemed quite satisfied with the turn
of events. I did notice, however, that they didn't start any
spontaneous conversations on the subject with me. And when I
expressed my doubts over certain charges against the Four
(particularly Chang Chun-chiao, Yao Wen-yuan, and Wan
Hung-wen — I didn't have so many doubts about those against
Chiang Ching!), I tended to get unsatisfying answers — although not for want of trying on their part. Even after (or
should I say especially after?) I was read large sections of the official Central Committee document "explaining" the case
against the Four (the document which the Chinese people had
been read in their workplaces sometime before the street
demonstrations), I still thought the charges pretty weak. My
response was to work out a list of some twenty detailed questions which I handed to the leadership of my work unit in written form. After a period of time one of my superiors came to
me and did his best to deal with the questions I had raised.
Again I was dissatisfied. Why couldn't I get clearcut answers to
what seemed to me to be clearcut questions? One possibility
was that those I was questioning didn't have much information

on the subject. Another was that we weren't speaking the same "language," weren't employing the same analytical framework.

I was more comfortable discussing my riddles with my wife and non-Chinese friends. At least they seemed to get the point of my questions, even if they too didn't always have convincing answers. We would discuss and argue far into the night. Some of my foreign friends, with much longer experience of China than I had under my belt, were able to shed light on things which were still little more than mysteries to me. Some of them had built up close comradeships with Chinese colleagues over the years, and were thus in a far better position to read prevailing moods than I was. Perhaps the greatest help my non-Chinese friends gave me in that early period was the assurance that the general public elation was not feigned, but real.

And I read. Everything I could get my hands on. But the official *People's Daily* used the same language to describe the Four and their "crimes" as it had used to condemn Teng Hsiao-ping not many months before. One could be forgiven for thinking that sometimes the articles were simply reruns with appropriate name changes made to take care of new circumstances. The *Hsinhua News Bulletins* carried article after article filled with seemingly wild charges, mostly relating to the alleged bizarre lifestyle and activities of the Four. These articles, too, were couched in the same heavy prose that had been used for years. For their part, *Peking Review* and *China Reconstructs* continued to dutifully reprint the Hsinhua material with a minimum of helpful annotation for their all-foreign audiences. Not surprisingly, such reading did little to alleviate my confusion.

But then one day somebody from Hsinhua News Agency dropped by to solicit my views on how to improve propaganda destined for foreign consumption. He was concerned—seriously it seemed—with the inability of his agency to communicate the momentous changes that were taking place in China in a way that would be convincing to foreign readers. He also expressed concern about the way in which his agency had been misused by the Four for their own purposes (Yao Wen-yuan, as you know, was the Politburo member responsible for the general overseeing of the various propaganda media). I gave the Hsinhua representative an earful about the problems with Chinese propaganda as I saw them, while he wrote it all down in his notebook. When I had finished he thanked me and went off to ask the opinion of the other foreign friends working here. About the same time, letters started appearing in the *People's Daily* criticizing its unreadability—and even its unreliability. More food for thought.

The *People's Daily* organization and Hsinhua News Agency are both huge outfits. Hsinhua (which provides most of the *People's Daily*'s basic news items) is responsible for gathering both world and national news, and for writing, translating, and reproducing enormous quantities of printed material every day. Its hundreds of staff writers have acquired a style of writing which will not be easily changed: not enough concrete facts; not much in the way of dialectical balance; mainly "safe," quotation-laden rhetoric. Part of the reason for this sorry state of affairs is that for several years these writers have had to cope with supervision by a few well-disguised, outwardly "radical" opportunists—ready to pounce on them for every political "error," real or supposed. A larger factor, however, is the widespread tendency to steer clear of any criticism of material that could possibly be claimed to embody the current concerns of Chairman Mao, however tenuous its relationship to those concerns might be, or however in need of criticism and improvement. Small wonder, then, that Hsinhua's propaganda has been found wanting at home as well as abroad. Small wonder that the needed changes won't take place overnight. But the Hsinhua leader who asked for my opinions was nonetheless sincere; the same goes for the *People's Daily* editors who chose to print the criticisms from their readers, something that hasn't been customary in recent years. Changes are taking place. For one thing, people who had simply given up looking at the *People's Daily* are reading it regularly once again. Perhaps you've even noticed some slight improvement in your *Peking Review!*

Time alone will tell how far and how fast the improvements in propaganda will go. But the fundamental point that needs to be made here is that propaganda is not "reality," merely one small part of it. And though its task should be to accurately and didactically portray the whole of reality, it is very easy for propaganda to slip into misrepresentation, as even a critical reading of *Le Monde* will attest. I believe that in the Chinese case, such misrepresentation as occurs today is generally unintentional. But the propaganda which helped you and me prepare our logical categories for the events of last fall was in rather large measure an intentional misrepresentation of the Chinese political scene. And who should take the blame for that? It clearly seems too simple to pin all the responsibility on Yao Wen-yuan or the Four and be done with it. Didn't the rest of the leadership ever read the *People's Daily?* Why did the media people go along with the falsifications? And what about their audiences?

About the responses of the leaders, not much can be said with certainty. We do know that Chairman Mao at least used to read the *People's Daily*, and that he was critical of both its style and content. Perhaps by the time the Four had helped it get into outright falsification, he, like the other people I mentioned above, had given up reading it, but I doubt this. As for the other leaders, I personally have no information on their reading habits. But in attempting to answer the question of why those directly responsible for the day-to-day content and style (the writers and editors) went along, we are on more solid ground and have a good deal of concrete evidence. Let me suggest that the line between overt manipulation for planned ends and the unintentional distortion in which the media people were already engaged was a rather fine one, one quite susceptible of being crossed unnoticed. If you go back over the written propaganda of the past several years, you won't find any sudden or startling discontinuities. There's no reason to believe that those engaged in its creation should have either. What some of them may have noticed was a little more direction from on high as to the "correct line"; a little more supervision over the selection of articles (a few more by "Liang Hsiao" and "Lo Ssu-ting," a few more by the "Joint Mass Criticism Group" of Peking and Tsinghua universities); a little more help on the drafting of major editorials (provision of the quotes embodying the most recent "concerns" of Chairman Mao, for instance). Who could complain? The increased attention by the representatives of the Central Committee was merely confirmation of the special importance placed on propaganda work. Wasn't it?

We've already partially answered the question about the final audience, members of the general public. There's no reason to suspect that they detected any major discontinuities in the *People's Daily* fare either. But we do know that the result of an extended diet was increasing uncertainty and confusion. The population at large was, after all, immersed in social reality. As the gap between what was written or heard (from official sources) and what was directly experienced widened—albeit imperceptibly—two things occurred. First, as I've already noted, there were fewer and fewer people reading and listening; and second, those who remained faithful had to exercise their powers of rationalization to a greater and greater degree.

Well, if the picture I've painted seems to you to be a deplorable one, at least the problems can't be attributed solely to the present leadership! In fact, if you can bring yourself to persist in your reading of the propaganda, you'll find that two of the "post-Four" themes have been opposition to stereotyped writing and the seeking of truth from facts. On the other hand, if you choose to extend your research in a more historical direction, it will lead you to somewhat more than an exposure of the Four. For example, if you were to examine the whole of the printed record from Liberation on, you'd find that there was one clear watershed, one unmistakable discontinuity, in journalistic style and content. It occurred in the late spring of 1966 —it was one of the products of the Great Proletarian Cultural Revolution. In other words, the Cultural Revolution did give rise to certain negative consequences, or (to put it another way) exacerbated negative tendencies which were already latent. Chairman Mao suggested that the negative consequences of the Cultural Revolution amounted to perhaps some 30 percent, the positive to perhaps 70 percent. You, as a dialectician and author of *Class Struggles in the USSR*, should not be surprised.

Another example. In your comments on China's foreign policy—a decidedly controversial topic abroad—you suggest that the struggle against the two superpowers has gradually been replaced by a struggle solely against social-imperialism. After amplifying on this rather dubious theme, you inform us that: "The present international practices of the Chinese Communist Party damage China's prestige with people, especially in the Third World." While it would be difficult to deny that among those with an inadequate grasp of dialectical materialism ("realism"?), China's practices in international affairs must seem baffling much of the time, they aren't, after all, so new. If you go back over your *Peking Reviews,* you'll see that an upsurge in the practices to which you refer is more or less coterminous with the beginning of the present decade. Such a reading will also suggest that, if Chou En-lai was the main day-to-day practitioner (before Teng was assigned the task), Mao Tse-tung was rather more than an unwilling onlooker. From the photos alone, one could amass compelling evidence of Chairman Mao's complicity. May I suggest to you, as Chinese propaganda has tried so hard to make clear, that not only was Chairman Mao a participant in what you describe as prestige-damaging practices; he was also the main architect of their underlying revolutionary strategy. It is perfectly legitimate to wonder whether the Chinese leadership hasn't made a few mistakes in its application of the grand vision, but if it has, then Chinese propaganda itself forces us to be even-handed in apportioning responsibility. As for China's loss of prestige among Third World peoples, one hardly gets the impression from propaganda available here that Third World leaders (even the progressive ones) are among those who are alleged to be losing respect for China.

I could go on in this vein, but I hesitate to bore you. I'll only mention that what may seem to you and me to be verbal "overkill" in dealing with the Four is not a new invention either. Again, *Peking Review* alone provides sufficient evidence. Consider the charges (and the verdicts) against Liu Shao-chi and Lin Piao. Were those charges also indicative of a "revisionist line"?

You can see that I am not saying that there was never any point in reading the various propaganda organs which China publishes. On the contrary, a tremendous amount can be gleaned from the foreign-language publications alone. Unfortunately, though, the most revealing articles are not always selected for translation, and those that are have sometimes been worked over by the editors of Hsinhua until much of their impact has been lost. A reading ability in Chinese helps one a long way toward understanding. Let me cite just one example. In your letter you state that: "The struggle against bourgeois right is scarcely mentioned any more." No regular readers of Chinese-language materials could possibly make such an assertion (and they might even question your use of the words "struggle against," believing that the issue is one of "restricting" bourgeois right, not "struggling against" it). I, for one, could provide you with a list of theoretical articles which have appeared in Chinese over the past year on precisely this subject. The latest such article to come to my attention is a relatively lengthy one by Li Hung-lin which was run just four days ago in the *People's Daily* of September 27. Among other things, it draws a clear line of distinction between bourgeois right, compensation according to labor, and outright illegal practices. We couldn't have drawn such clear lines two years ago; theory has been advancing.

Let us move on. If Chinese propaganda has not always been noticeably more reliable than Western establishment propaganda about China (at least in the recent past), neither have either of them been the only sources of information available to those who really seek to understand. There have always been the reports of "independent" observers with varying degrees of access to both leaders and common citizens. There have always been the officially (and unofficially) published verbatim texts of various keynote speeches and policy documents. These sources are all available to you in Paris and, as your various publications suggest, you are aware of their inherent strengths and weaknesses. Independent observers are not necessarily "objective" observers, but as a Marxist you should know how to take account of their biases. Speeches and party and government documents have their specific problems too, but your thoroughgoing familiarity with Soviet documentation has surely made you aware of the difference between a leader's or leadership's limited understanding and honest mistakes on the one hand, and conscious deceit on the other.

Let me give you but one example of what you might learn from such sources. Consider the issue of bourgeois right once again. The speech of Vice-Premier Yu Chiu-li delivered at last spring's National Taching Conference (*Peking Review*, no. 22, 1977), while not adding much to the theoretical discussion of bourgeois right, did have several things to say about it of an immediately practical nature. If you refer to section five of that speech, you will see that Vice-Premier Yu issued a call for the enlarging of the very public services which help to reduce the disparities and hardships resulting from the continued existence of bourgeois right. Of course, if you are one of those who thinks that the bourgeois right problem could be "solved" simply by taking something away from those who are relatively well off or whose needs are less in order to give it to those whose needs are greater, then you won't be satisfied with my example. But then, neither would you be taking cognizance of the extreme tensions, even large-scale strife, that such a policy would entail. (Which superagency, after all, would be entrusted with making what many would consider rather arbitrary decisions concerning "needs"?) Whatever your views, bourgeois right will be restricted, is being restricted, in the manner Yu Chiu-li advocates, and the effects will undoubtedly quicken as the forces of production grow. By way of contrast, the lack of interest in—or do you prefer "inability to offer"?— practical steps toward solution by Yao Wen-yuan and Chang Chun-chiao, our favorite theoreticians, was not missed by the masses.

This brings us to my next point. Propaganda, independent reports, speeches, and documents are all likely to come to your attention via the printed word unless you are able to catch Radio Peking. This means that, even though you may be adept at "reading between the lines," there will be no real dialogue, no chance to pick up some of those tell-tale signs which help us establish an attitude—perhaps an empathy—toward a living informant. Historians generally have to be satisfied with printed sources and whatever random artifacts remain which shed light on their subject. They have to try to breathe life back into them. As a historian of the early years of the Russian Revolution, you will know the problem well. We may be able to feel that we really "know" Lenin after we've read widely in the forty or so volumes of his collected works, but we're bound to feel less familiar with most of the other early Soviet leaders. But even when we can't meet and talk with high-ranking leaders in the flesh, can we not still learn a lot from those who have had such opportunities? Or from those who have been, in one sense, the object of those leaders' policy decisions and guidance over an extended period of time? I dare say that your work on the Soviet Union would have been far less useful to your readers had you never visited that country, worked there, gained a first-hand familiarity with some of its people, achievements, problems. Perhaps even today you are able to maintain some direct contact with certain facets of Soviet life. If so, that contact is bound to help you in your writing of the second and third volumes of your opus, and make them better books.

For the above reasons, it is indeed surprising that your letter of resignation conveys no hint that there would be any useful purpose served in coming into contact now with aspects of Chinese reality other than the printed ones I've discussed. Since we are not dealing with past history here, but rather with contemporary events, this omission is virtually unintelligible to me. I do know that you have been a visitor to China several times in the past. I'm not certain, but I suspect, that you neither read nor speak Chinese. But do you really feel that nothing further could be learned by coming here once more? Do you feel that the language problem is an insurmountable barrier to talking to those Chinese who might answer the particular doubts you have? Or is it that you've succumbed to the idea currently flowing in French sinological circles that the rules concerning contact with foreigners and the fantastic organizational and disciplinary talents of the Chinese authorities would prevent you from coming into contact here with anything other than variations of the "official line"? If it's one or any combination of these reasons, I can only say that you are the victim of metaphysical thinking. All these possible considerations harbor an element of truth. But, in essence, they are wrong—without exception.

Let me suggest how a couple of the points raised in your letter might be seen in a new light after even a brief visit here. Firstly, if you were taken on even a "standard" tour of some factory of your choice (say, for the sake of example, the printing plant of the Foreign Languages Press), during the customary question period you might raise the seeming contradiction concerning the falsification of photographs. The answers given to you by your hosts might vary in detail, but I think that the gist of them would be that the appearance of leaders in, or their removal from, photos is basically a matter of general approval, or strong disapproval, of those leaders and their political lines. You could reply that this was nonsense, that any photograph is only a reflection of a factual occurrence. I have good reason to believe that you would be met with disagreement, and perhaps with the additional information that had anybody tried to force the printers to print unaltered photos of the leadership lineup at the funeral services for Chairman Mao in *China Reconstructs*, *Peking Review*, or *China Pictorial*, there would have been forceful obstruction by the printers themselves. If you got frustrated with this line of argument and asked bluntly why, then, Hsinhua could be so self-righteous in calling the very same technique dastardly when carried out at the Four's behest, you would be pointedly reminded which individual's images the Four had excised. On the other hand, if you went into a soliloquy on mystification and false consciousness, some sophisticate among your hosts might turn the matter around at you and put you on the spot about publishing and editing habits in France. Finally, if you threw up your hands in despair and wondered aloud how history could have any meaning at all, your listeners would probably not understand your dilemma—or if they did, might reply that history is the business of archivists and historians, that the practice in question concerned not "history," but current class struggle, and that no decent historian could aspire to illustrate a work with photographs of such despicable people as the Four in any case. (Incidentally, the recent publication of some of the very photos which the Four are accused of tampering with imparts a certain validity to the point about the job of archivists, if not historians; the negatives were never destroyed.)

Now, you might initially walk away from such an exchange feeling that the only plausible explanation of such "irrational" replies was that you had been dealing with hosts with a particularly low level of theoretical understanding; but after putting the same "contradiction" to other hosts on subsequent occasions and getting variations on the same theme in reply, you'd have to choose between two possible explanations (leaving aside the third possibility that it was your hosts who were correct and your view that was in error). One of the possible explanations would be that your informants had been methodically briefed ahead of time on everything known about you and your doubts—and on what their answers should be to every conceivable question that you might ask. That choice would, I think, be preposterous. The other possible explanation would be that you were simply being confronted with an objective fact, namely, that with regard to photographs of leaders there is a widespread idea in China which doesn't correspond with an equally widespread idea prevalent in some of the other countries with which you are acquainted. As a Marxist, you would have to take this fact, couple it with relevant related facts, and subject the whole to analysis, using methods with which you are familiar. But I can't for the life of me see how either choice would help you to conclude that a revisionist line predominates at present—as opposed to, say, two years ago, or ten years ago. If you require proof of my point, look back at the photos in your *China Reconstructs* issues of 1967 and 1968. You'd certainly be hard-pressed to blame the practice of falsification on any single group of leaders.

A second area of doubt which you would be forced to reexamine if you were to visit China today concerns what you call in your letter "slander and scandal," "unbelievable accusations," and "gross falsifications." Again, any investigation which you made here would inevitably bring you into contact with some of the originators of the stories to which you have attached such strong labels. You would then find that those responsible weren't just the leaders who had a hand in putting down the Four last October; nor were they fiction writers in the employ of a diabolical press. You'd probably have to admit that the majority of them were rather ordinary working people or lower-level cadres of one kind or another. Excluding the possibility that they are all thoroughly opportunist individuals, great liars and fine actors, you'd probably also have to take at least some of their stories seriously. These people claim either to have witnessed activities of the Four that were far removed from anything that they, the onlookers, could rationalize as socialist morality, or they claim to have personally been victims of repression by the Four. Some of the story-tellers would express themselves in language which would convince you that they had more than a casual acquaintance with Marxism.

If you were to question these people about why they hadn't spoken out immediately—at the time of the events they witnessed or experienced—you'd get several answers. Some of your informants would tell you that they had indeed spoken out and had suffered because of it. Others, probably a small minority, would tell you that they too had spoken out, but had been protected by their comrades and organizations from retaliation by the Four. But perhaps the majority would tell you that fear of repression had stilled their tongues. Whatever the case, if you persisted in your investigations and checked out the stories you had been told, you'd find that at least some of them were well known and believed by large numbers of people long before October of last year—not through the official media, of course, but through what's known here as "lane-news": word-of-mouth.

Again you'd have to make a choice. Either you'd continue to maintain that the accusations against the Four were just "slander and scandal," that is, unrelated to their "line," to their socialism, to their practice; or you'd have to accept that they were part of the relevant evidence on judging the accused.

If you chose the former, it seems to me that you'd be suggesting that socialist practice is akin to an eight-to-five work shift— that what people do "on their own time" is their business so long as they maintain acceptable standards while "on the job." If you chose the latter (that these stories are relevant evidence), you'd be in step with the majority of Chinese. In either case, you'd have to accept another objective fact: that there is a widespread belief in this country that the stories are true, that the conduct related in them isn't socialist, and that the Four are guilty as accused. Again, you'd have to analyze this fact in conjunction with others. Again, I can't see how your analysis could lead you to the conclusion that a revisionist line predominates at present—as opposed to, say, three and a half years ago. And again, if you require proof of my point, peruse some of the propaganda about Lin Piao published in 1974 or, better yet, recall some of the stories you were told about Lin and his cohorts during your last trip here.

The foregoing line of argument leads us to another fundamental problem. What role does the consciousness—do the ideas—of the masses play during the period of socialist transition? Your letter might lead one to think they're irrelevant, even though I'm fairly certain that you would be quick to agree, in any theoretical discussion, that the raising of mass consciousness was central to Mao Tse-tung's whole approach to revolutionary transformation. Let's look at the matter more closely.

Mass consciousness—or if you like, class consciousness—at any given point in time is an objective historical fact. Of course, any consciousness is also a dynamic, changing entity as well. But for purposes of analysis and planning we have no alternative but to stop it, catch it, describe it. And when we do it is what it is, nothing more or less; it is idealist nonsense to talk about what it "should be" or what we "wish" it were, at the moment of apprehension. As dialecticians, we can't forget that it's possible to talk in general terms about how it will develop, or even how it "should" be developed, but we must admit that we can't know what "fully developed" proletarian consciousness means. (In fact, no such thing will ever exist, and only a metaphysician thinks that it can.) Nevertheless, we do know rather a lot today about the nature of its developmental process. Now, we could ever so easily slip into the ongoing argument over how closely consciousness is tied to the development of the forces of production, which factor is the leading factor, and so on, but I for one don't have anything new to add to the theoretical controversy at the moment. My purpose in raising the issue lies elsewhere.

My point is that the aim of correctly apprehending the content and level of mass consciousness at any given point in time is to provide the necessary data for building and advancing a strategy for revolutionary transformation. Such a strategy can only be as good as the data is accurate. A materialist can't afford to think otherwise. Now you may be convinced that you hold the truth on such matters as tampering with news photos (I tend to think you do) and "slander and scandal" (I tend to think you don't), but you're nevertheless confronted with objective facts in the form of widespread disagreement with your views on those subjects here in China. Similarly, the Four *may* have been convinced that they held the keys to desirable revolutionary transformations of Chinese society, but it seems that, at least in recent years, they couldn't convince the masses—or keep them convinced.

Minority conviction confronts mass "recalcitrance." Seemingly "advanced Marxism" confronts popular inertia. Which gives way? The bourgeois answer is ambiguous: either the minority "should" accede to the wishes of the majority, or those in error "should" accede to those who are correct. The Marxist answer is: neither "gives way." The convinced minority tries to create, or at least describe, a practice that will be convincing to the masses (a description perhaps of the concrete effect on foreign readers of the photos in question?). The vanguard Marxists (if they are really scientific Marxists) try to set up a convincing, limited-scale demonstration, or to otherwise provide the conditions under which the masses can see the validity of the new truths, see their inherent advantages, adopt them as their own. May I be permitted just one quotation from Mao Tse-tung?

The Central Committee has emphasized time and again that the masses must educate themselves and liberate themselves. This is because world outlook cannot be imposed upon them. In order to transform ideology [consciousness], it is necessary for the external causes to function through the inner causes, though the latter are principal.   (August 31, 1967)

We have now come to the last major problem I wish to deal with, namely, the relationship of leaders to led, to the masses. Your letter implies, though it does not directly state, that it is the present Communist Party leaders who are responsible for the revisionist line which is supposedly triumphing. One can also infer that you believe that this revisionist line would not presently be dominant if the Four were "in power" (or at least sharing "power"). I have tried to show through several examples that the present leadership is far from being solely responsible for certain of the things which you condemn and which make up part of your case for a revisionist line. My objective has not been to cast doubt on Chairman Mao (not even on what you call his "vigilance"); nor has it been to indict all China's leaders in some measure or other. It has rather been to restore some of the links between China's leaders and those they lead—between leaders and the general sociopolitical environment—that were so lamentably absent from your letter. I can only assume that the omission is a reflection of some basic shortcomings in your deepest vision of leadership.

Do you really believe that China's top leaders should exercise direct control over every aspect of the day-to-day life and work of the Chinese people? Do you believe such a thing possible? Do you really believe that the Chinese leaders should—or could— simply impose their views, however Marxist-Leninist, advanced, scientific, or trouble-saving they might be? Or, to be more specific, should Politburo members veto every article that Hsinhua News Agency turns out? Should Chairman Mao have saved everybody the confusion, the agony—and the education —of the last few years by simply dismissing the Four personally? (If so, then why not Liu Shao-chi in, say, 1962; or Lin Piao in, say, 1969?) Should he have saved everybody the confusion, the agony—and the education—of the Cultural Revolution as well? Should the Four simply have kept right on sticking recalcitrants under detention until those not in confinement submitted to their "advanced Marxism-Leninism"? I am sure that you don't, in fact, believe these things, for some of them smack more of fascism than of the socialism to which you are committed. And yet, by stretching the imagination ever so little, it would be possible to draw such conclusions from positions taken in your letter.

Your books, however, are quite another matter. From them one gets the impression that you understand that the pre-eminent socialist leaders — leaders such as Lenin and Mao — have been those who had developed that all-too-rare ability to look at a complex event or process, draw out its essence or sum up its main trend, and then feed back into the overall reality, of which it is a part, in a positive way. But concretely, what is that "positive way"? It's the one which helps the real makers of history, the masses, advance; the one which helps them to educate themselves, liberate themselves, transform their own ideology.

If what I have said here is correct, then the essence of real leadership is a pedagogical one: the finest leaders are nothing more than the best teachers. Not the ones who act as though they have a monopoly on understanding. Not the ones who try to cram students with facts or theory which they can't, because of limited experience, really grasp. Not the ones who think that a dose of terror helps promote the learning process. Not even the paternalistic ones who subconsciously fear the day when "their" students will become sufficiently independent to get along without their own direct tutelage. Rather, I'm thinking of those teachers who see their own knowledge as a trust from the people, see the learning process as a mutual experience, encourage the building of self-discipline and hard work through their own example, and whose greatest happiness comes from seeing those with whom they've been exploring and changing the world around them go off to carry on the process with others.

Mao Tse-tung will always be known to revolutionary people, both in China and the world over, as the "Great Leader and

Teacher." Whatever else they may be called, not one of the Four is ever likely to be thought of as a "teacher" of the masses. As for members of the present leadership, we shall have to wait and see. But we must remember that many of the circumstances which created a Mao Tse-tung no longer prevail in China; new circumstances, new challenges, exist. Let's not be surprised to find that individual working styles vary from leader to leader. And let's not be too quick to label those who don't quite measure up to the ideal profile I've sketched above as "revisionists," "capitalist-roaders," or what have you. On the other hand, let's not fail to recognize good leadership when we are confronted with it.

I'd like to suggest to you that the present leadership has, in fact, moved rather rapidly to create—recreate—the essential conditions under which the masses can continue to educate themselves and liberate themselves. It has already gone a long way toward removing the uncertainty, confusion, and fear of arbitrary maltreatment which large numbers of the Chinese people have been experiencing as "real" phenomena in recent years, and which these same people are convinced were largely the responsibility of the Four. It is at this very moment implementing new regulations to alleviate the economic insecurity of city-dwellers in the lowest income categories through a readjustment of wage scales. It has brought socialist emulation out from under the cloud of the "theory of productive forces." All these steps, and others yet to come, are positive, and can only lead to a new outpouring of mass initiative.

As for the tools needed by the masses for their self-education and self-liberation, the present leaders can hardly be faulted. Look at the facts. They have initiated a crash program for the publication of Mao Tse-tung's major works. They have reconfirmed and further popularized the models—Tachai and Taching—with which Chairman Mao's name was so closely identified, and they have reaffirmed the approach to operating socialist enterprises—the Anyang Charter—which Chairman Mao endorsed. Most importantly, they have written the standards of behavior for party members into a new party constitution, have devised certain institutions for seeing that those standards are upheld, and have done their best to make sure that the standards are known to the entire population.

I personally believe that the moves which I've enumerated here are not the methods of revisionists. But, as in the past, perhaps there are major flaws in my logical system and categories, and perhaps I'll ultimately be proven wrong. For one thing, like you, I can't know the magnitude of the forces opposed to the present political course. But whether I'm right or wrong, of one thing I'm certain: it is history and the masses that must be the judge.

The People's Republic of China is twenty-eight years old today. In some senses, Chinese society is a more complex, dynamic social organism than it was on October 1, 1949. It is by no means a perfect society. While the main trend is, I think, "fast forward," there's some retrogression too. But that in itself is nothing new. The class struggle goes on, for the moment largely in connection with various sins attributed to the Four. In your letter you raise the specter of the advances of the Cultural Revolution being wiped away. Some of its products will indeed be dropped, others modified—some for the right reasons, some not. And since classes and class struggle are going to be with us for some time to come, it's even conceivable that a revisionist line—a real revisionist line—might gain the upper hand for a time someday, through *coup d'état*, intrigue, power struggle, or whatever (the name doesn't really matter), and attempt to sweep it all away. But could the really important gains of the Cultural Revolution ever be submerged for long? Not a chance! They're in our very blood. They've inspired your books. They infuse Chairman Hua Kuo-feng's speeches. Without them, I couldn't have written this letter. And armed with them, the Chinese masses have the major weapon they need to combat a revisionist line should one come along.

I would be most happy to stand corrected on any errors I have made in interpreting the substance of your letter, and to receive criticism on any of the points I've set forth here. Though I've never had the opportunity to meet you, in the past I've always thought of you as one of my teachers. It is for this reason that I hope you'll accept my criticisms in the spirit in which they are offered. I'd like to hope, too, that you'll reconsider the positions set forth in your letter, and the assumptions which underlie your doubts; that you'll find it possible to continue to make your contribution as a supporter— a critical supporter— of the present leadership. As for those with whom you've had disagreements over the events of the past year, it's their duty to encourage you in these endeavors and, if you have a change of heart, to welcome you back without reservation.

Yours sincerely,
Neil G. Burton

THE GREAT LEAP BACKWARD
by Charles Bettelheim

March 3, 1978

"The history of all hitherto
existing society is the history of
class struggles"
— Karl Marx and
Friedrich Engels,
*Manifesto of the
Communist Party*

Dear Neil Burton,

I read your letter of October 1, 1977, with great interest,
and if I have not replied to it sooner this is because I was
unable to do so owing to previous commitments. This is also
the reason (together with health considerations) why I was
unable to agree to go to China last year.

In your letter you say that if I had visited China again in
1977, I would not have come to the conclusions which I set out
in my letter resigning the presidency of the Franco-Chinese
Friendship Association. I do not agree at all. First, because the
documents which are now being published in China give
expression to a certain *political line*, and it is *the existence of
this line* which has led me to the conclusions I have drawn.
Secondly, because, both before and since I wrote that letter, I
have met many travelers just back from China—friends of
China, sinologists, former students or teachers from abroad
who were working in China, journalists, and so on—and what
they have told me about their experiences (even when they
themselves approve of the current political line) has confirmed
me in my conclusions. In the following pages I take into

account, of course, both recently published documents and the conversations I have had, since I resigned, with travelers who have since returned. These different elements have enabled me, I believe, to grasp better the significance of what has happened in China. My letter thus seeks to be more than a mere reply to yours: it is a first attempt at systematic thinking about the political changes which have taken place in China since October 1976 and about the conditions which prepared the way for them.

Instead of going over again, point by point, the arguments in my letter of last year, or answering, point by point, what you wrote to me on October 1, 1977, I prefer to explain how I analyze the present situation and the events that have produced it, for matters have now become clearer than they were: in particular, it is more obvious *what policy has triumphed* as a result of the elimination of the Four, namely, a bourgeois policy and not a proletarian one.

In the following pages I shall try, also, to explain the reasons why, in my opinion, the situation has evolved in the way it has. I think that by proceeding in this way I shall be able to reply to the best of my ability to the letter you wrote me.

The End of the Cultural Revolution

The first question that needs to be examined is that of the relation between the present situation and the Cultural Revolution. On this point we must note straightaway that the leadership of the Chinese Communist Party has now proclaimed that the Cultural Revolution is ended. This statement is certainly correct. It amounts to a recognition that a change has taken place in the relation between social and political forces, resulting in the extreme restriction of the activity of the masses, and of the freedom of initiative and expression that the Cultural Revolution was to have enabled them to conquer.

In fact, when we look back and analyze what has happened since 1965-66, we can say that this change in the relation of forces was already apparent in the first months of 1967 (when the political form of the Shanghai Commune was created and then abandoned),[1] and that thereafter it continued, with zigzags in the same direction. The announcement of the end of the Cultural Revolution was thus the culmination of a historical process that lasted for several years, a process of class struggle requiring protracted analysis. The way in which this announcement took place calls for two observations.

It is to be noted, first, that the announcement was not accompanied by any systematic striking of the balance of the Cultural Revolution as a whole. The failure to do this means that no distinction has been made by the new leadership of the Chinese Communist Party between changes of a positive kind, from the standpoint of the working people, which have taken place thanks to the Cultural Revolution, and those changes or practices that may have had negative consequences. *The door is thus left open for a de facto challenge to everything contributed by the Cultural Revolution.* This is so even though *homage is paid, in words,* to the Cultural Revolution, and it is said that there will be other such revolutions. Without a clear analysis of the past, as thoroughgoing as possible, it is very difficult to find one's way correctly in the future.

Secondly, alongside the announcement that the Cultural Revolution is over, the measures which have been taken since more than a year ago, and the themes expounded in official speeches and in the press, constitute a de facto negation of the Cultural Revolution. There has been a veritable *leap backward.* These two aspects of the present situation are obviously not accidental. They are the product of profound tendencies, the result of a certain *relation of forces between classes* and also of a *political line* which forms part of this relation of forces and reacts upon it.

I expect that you disagree with the formulations I have just set forth, so I shall develop my line of argument. This argument can, of course, only be partial; for it to be otherwise one would need to do what the Chinese Communist Party has not done, namely, to undertake the striking of a systematic balance of the Cultural Revolution as a whole, recalling the aims that were proclaimed at the outset, estimating the extent to which there were advances and retreats, and analyzing why they occurred. Such a task could be accomplished only by a political organization linked with the masses. It would also require a number of documents and items of information which I do not possess—and which a stay in China would not, of course, enable me to collect, because, where many points are concerned, what is involved is documents and information that it is considered need to be kept "secret."

This being so, what I propose to do is to reveal certain aspects of the leap backward effected in recent months, and then to consider the reasons for it. Before doing that, however, it is necessary to recall some of the proclaimed intentions of the Cultural Revolution, especially those which constituted a sharp turn away from previous practices—intentions which, at certain periods, became more or less realized in Chinese life, and which are now being challenged.

The Problem of Mass Democracy

When we study the "Sixteen-Point Decision" adopted on August 8, 1966, by the Central Committee of the Chinese Communist Party, we see that one of the fundamental aims it proclaimed was to promote the development of a political line that would enable the masses to express themselves freely, without being subjected to constraint when expressing minority views, "even if the minority is wrong" (point 6 of the "Sixteen-Point Decision"). The activity of the masses was to be allowed to assume many different organizational forms and to lead to the formation of organs of power in the factories, mines, and enterprises, in the various quarters of the cities and in the villages, in the state organizations, and in educational establishments. All this activity was to culminate in "a system of general elections like that of the Paris Commune." The elected members were to be continuously criticized by those who had elected them, and could be replaced or recalled by the masses (point 9). This aim was not seen as being merely provisional in character, for its "great historic importance" was emphasized. An essential principle was also recalled (since it had not been honored in the preceding period), namely, that "the only method is for the masses to liberate themselves, and any method of doing things on their behalf must not be used"; the masses must educate themselves in the movement" (point 4). In accordance with this principle, the party can play its role only by not hesitating to promote the activity of the masses. The party leaders at every level must therefore encourage the masses to criticize the shortcomings and mistakes in their own work (point 3).

At the same time, it was said that criticisms ought to be made in a spirit of unity and with a view to rectifying mistakes rather than eliminating those who had committed them. Finally, what was to be aimed at was "to achieve the unity of more than 95 percent of the cadres and more than 95 percent of the masses" (point 5).

One of the purposes proclaimed was the transformation of the superstructure, in which bourgeois ideology continued to bulk large, so that, in particular, it was necessary to "transform education, literature, art, etc." (points 1 and 10).

The link between the struggle for revolution and the struggle for production was also mentioned, and it was stressed that priority should be given to the former.

From 1966 onward, a movement developed that underwent ebbs and flows which need to be analyzed if one is fully to comprehend the present situation, but, as I have said already, such an analysis cannot be made in any detail at present. This movement also had its ideological and theoretical aspects. It led Mao Tse-tung and those who are today being vilified by the present leadership of the party to recognize in practice the difference between changing the juridical ownership of enterprises and changing the relations of production and distribution, so that a series of statements appeared which pointed out that it was possible for capitalist enterprises to exist "behind a socialist signboard," that the wage system prevailing in China was not very different from capitalism, that the bourgeoisie was present in the party, and so on.

One has only to read the Chinese press today to see that, since Mao's death, the intentions of the Cultural Revolution and the theoretical developments which accompanied it are being more and more openly abandoned. The so-called criticism of the Four serves as a pretext for this abandonment.[2]

The Leap Backward Effected Since the End of 1976

As I have said, the retreat from the proclaimed objectives of the Cultural Revolution did not begin at the end of 1976. It had begun much earlier, in connection with the ebb and flow of the class struggle. Nevertheless, the period which opened with the death of Mao Tse-tung and the elimination of the Four has been marked by the extent to which the *leap backward* has been accomplished and by the open abandonment of a series of analyses developed since 1966. This abandonment means a repudiation of the gains made for Marxism by the Chinese Revolution — in other words, a *repudiation of Marxism itself*.

As regards the ebbs that occurred before Mao's death, I shall confine myself to recalling a few facts. I have already mentioned the dropping of the political form of the Shanghai Commune, which was replaced by the revolutionary committees, set up after 1967. But these committees themselves gradually withered. This withering proceeded in several ways: the principle of revocability of the committee members by the masses, and their periodic re-election, was respected less and less, the authority of the committees was gradually encroached upon by that of the corresponding party committees, and the frequent confusion of functions by those who belonged to both committees tended to deprive the revolutionary committees of their role of democratically expressing the aspirations and initiatives of the masses they were supposed to represent.

The same process of withering affected other organs that issued from the first years of the Cultural Revolution. Thus, the workers' management groups I wrote about in *Cultural Revolution and Industrial Organization in China* went to sleep. When I returned to China in the autumn of 1975, there was only one factory where I heard anything about these groups (after I had insisted on knowing whether such groups existed as I did in all the factories I visited), and what I was told left me with the impression that they were there only as ghosts, while everywhere else they seemed to have vanished completely.

This withering signified a step back in relation to the requirements for progress toward socialism, for that presupposes that the working people themselves become to an increasing extent masters, collectively, of their own conditions of life and labor. This step back did not happen "by itself." It resulted from class struggle, from the resurgent influence of the bourgeoisie, and above all of the bourgeoisie present in the machinery of the state and of the party, who were tending to strengthen their authority, to "free themselves" from the authority of the masses, and so to be able to dispose of the means of production which, in a formal sense, belong to the state.

In 1976, however, this retreat could still be seen as the effect of a momentary ebb, for *the Cultural Revolution was still the order of the day* and *a number of analyses were still being made* which clarified (even if not always thoroughly) the prerequisites for a revolutionary change in production relations and class relations. Today the situation is different, and we see a bourgeois and revisionist counteroffensive proceeding on all fronts: on the front of practical measures and concrete decisions, and on the front of ideological positions.

The Revolutionary Committees in the Production Units and the Strengthening of One-Man Management

This counteroffensive is aimed especially at what remains of the revolutionary committees *at the level of the production units*. It also seeks to *strengthen one-man management* and the *exclusive role of the party committee*, the different forms of *"three-in-one combination"* groups, and the *tightening of labor regulations and labor discipline*.

One of the first overt manifestations of the counteroffensive was the speech delivered on January 31, 1977, by Pai Ju-ping, first secretary of the Shantung Party Committee (broadcast by Radio Tsinan on February 1, 1977). Among the themes expounded in this speech (and which have reappeared since in numberless speeches by the highest authorities), we find that of the need to *strengthen the role of the party committees in the economic sphere, with nothing said about the tasks of the revolutionary committees.* In this speech, as in many others, not a word was said about the free expression of criticism by the workers. On the contrary, the speaker denounced criticisms which had been sent to the party committees, and placed one-sided emphasis on *obedience.* If he declared that "we must rely on the working class," this was *not because of that class's spirit of initiative* but because *"it is strictest in observing discipline and obeying orders."*

As I have said, these ideas are now being put forward more and more frequently. Thus, on April 6, 1977, Radio Peking stated: "In a socialist enterprise the relation between the party and other organizations is that between a guide and his disciples." Here, too, it is no longer a question of the initiative of the masses, or of learning from the masses. The sole wielder of authority is the party committee. The workers have only to let themselves be guided.

Anything that favors initiative on the part of the masses and of whatever is left of their organizations is denounced as corresponding to the "road of economism, syndicalism, anarchism, and radical individualism." Control exercized over the leaders is treated as breach of discipline, and the Four are criticized specifically for developing the idea of a contradiction between proletariat and bourgeoisie inside the factories, and speaking of antagonism between management and masses (New China News Agency [NCNA], May 21, 1977).

We thus see the revival of a doctrine that Mao Tse-tung rightly condemned, namely, that of the primacy of unity over contradiction, a doctrine characteristic of the ideology of the Soviet Communist Party in Stalin's time.

The ideology now being developed tends to *place the cadres and technicians above the workers* and to subject the latter to the authority of *regulations* composed by the former.

Factory "Despotism"

What we are watching is, in fact, a massive counteroffensive aimed at sweeping away everything that was said and done against the existence of oppressive regulations in the factories (what were called "unreasonable regulations").

It is now declared that these regulations (which it is indeed recognized, though only in passing, are determined by production relations) "reflect the objective laws governing the complex processes of modern large-scale production." The working class must therefore accept these regulations, since they reflect "objective laws." And Engels is brought in for support, by quoting a formulation which he put forward in a polemic against anarchism. In this work, written in 1873 and entitled *On Authority*, Engels wrote: "If man, by dint of his knowledge and inventive genius, has subdued the forces of nature, the latter avenge themselves upon him by subjecting him, insofar as he employs them, to a veritable despotism independent of all social organization. Wanting to abolish authority in large-scale industry is tantamount to wanting to abolish industry itself, to destroy the power loom in order to return to the spinning wheel."[3]

As Harry Braverman rightly points out, where Engels speaks of a "despotism independent of all social organization" and uses the concept of "authority" in a suprahistorical way, he allows himself to be carried away by his polemic. He thus loses sight of everything Marx wrote about the *socially determined character of "factory despotism."*[4] The use being made of this passage from Engels shows that what is being carried out in China today is, precisely, the *strengthening of despotism in the factory*—in the name of transhistorical "laws."

What we see here is not just a "theoretical consideration," but an attempt to justify the strengthening of repressive practices employed in relation to the workers. From now on, increasingly, growth in production, in the output and quality of goods, is expected to result, in the main, not from development of worker's initiative, organization, and consciousness, but from the *enforcement of strict regulations*. Thus, on August 14, 1977, Radio Peking said: "Rules and regulations ought never to be eliminated. Moreover, with the development of production and technology, rules and regulations must become stricter, and people must follow them precisely." Commenting on that last sentence, the speaker added: "This is a law of nature [!]. As production develops, so must we establish rules and regulations that are stricter and more rational." A prospect to inspire enthusiasm!

Criticism of the Four serves, among other things, as a pretext for advocating stricter regulations. Already in 1976 Yao Wen-yuan had criticized the idea of increasingly severe regulations. He wrote: "How far are we to go in this severity? Are we to introduce the capitalist mode of production, which even keeps check on the time the workers spend when they go to the toilet?"

From then on there was to be no more hesitation in praising "certain bourgeois rules and regulations" and "certain aspects of the way capitalist enterprises are managed," even to the point of saying that "these result from the workers' experience, and are therefore scientific"![5]

The pretext for strengthening what Marx called "factory despotism" is, on the one hand, the allegedly bad situation of the Chinese economy "in consequence of the activity of the Four," and, on the other, the "requirements" of the "four modernizations" (industrial, agricultural, military, and scientific-and-technological). I shall come back to these questions and their significance later. For the moment I want to emphasize particularly that it is in the name of these "requirements" that "emulation campaigns" are being set afoot — a development about which something needs to be said.

The Emulation Campaigns

I want, first of all, to make the point that the Soviet experience of the 1930s, and China's experience of the period preceding the Cultural Revolution, showed that *as soon as emulation ceases to result from a genuine movement of the masses* and becomes *a "campaign" organized from above,* it ceases to be in any way "socialist." It becomes a means whereby the cadres and technicians *exert pressure on the workers* in order to increase the intensity and productivity of labor. Such a campaign strips the workers even further of any control they may have over their conditions of labor, and so expropriates and exploits them even more than before. During the Cultural Revolution campaigns of this sort were not launched, but this did not prevent various forms of emulation from being developed in certain workshops, factories, mines, etc.

It was apparently in March 1977 that "emulation campaigns" had started in China. This happened after the national conference on the railways when it was announced that: "The experience of establishing great order and rapidly improving work on the railways is valid for all other departments and fronts" (NCNA, March 12, 1977). *Jen-min Jih-pao* of March 10 also issued a call for emulation campaigns. On March 22 that paper explained that emulation campaigns serve to establish "great order" and obtain "rapid results," raising productivity and output as quickly as possible by increasing labor discipline.

The character of these campaigns as movements which are *centralized* and *organized from above* is clearly apparent in a dispatch from NCNA dated January 7, 1978, which states that, with a view to "accelerated expansion of coal production, the Ministry of Coal Mining . . . has recently organized 125 of the country's mines in an emulation movement to last one hundred days, starting on January 1."

This dispatch explains that the ministry *requires* that the mines participating in the campaign "go all out to mobilize the masses and set up a *strong command network* as a measure aimed at accomplishing within one hundred consecutive days their tasks of coal-getting, in respect of quantity, quality, consumption, cost of production, and other production norms." The mines are invited to beat the record for all corresponding periods.

It could not be put more plainly that this "emulation campaign" is destined to subject the workers to a "command net work" and compel them not merely to fulfill the norms (fixed by the authorities) but also to beat production "records."

Campaigns like these have nothing in common with real socialist emulation. They fit in, moreover, with a whole political line which "restores the commanding role" to the economy, to production and profit. In relation to the principles of the Cultural Revolution period this represents a 180-degree turn. At the level of formulations, nothing gives better expression to this turn than a phrase used in a Radio Peking broadcast: "Politics must serve economics" (November 27, 1977).

Profit, Accumulation, and Concentration of Managerial Power Within the Enterprises

What a formulation like this implies has been made clear by a series of documents and declarations that have appeared since the end of 1976, all of them stressing the role of profit. Thus, issue no. 8 of 1977 of *Hung Chi* emphasizes above all the idea that enterprises must increase their profits and accumulate more funds for the state. It even says: "Asking whether one should run a factory for profit *or* for the revolution is a strange question." As if that could not be the actual source of contradictions, and as if it was not necessary to define the principal aspect of this contradiction!

Again, this article in *Hung Chi* states: "The more profit that a socialist enterprise makes in this way [i.e., by increasing production, practicing strict economy, raising the productivity of labor, and reducing costs], the more wealth it creates for socialism." It is thus assumed that the use made of the accumulated funds is automatically advantageous to socialism. And, above all, it is not even conceived that, in the struggle to increase profit (in which workers' initiative, the role of workers' management, and mass innovations are practically no longer mentioned), the leading role of the working class may eventually be repudiated. Yet when this leading role ceases, the doctrine that "making more profit means creating more wealth for socialism" becomes meaningless—and becomes, moreover, the same thesis that the Soviet revisionists have been repeating for years.

The editorial in *Jen-min Jih-pao* of August 27, 1977, tries, without being explicit about it, to "get rid" of this problem. This it does in a confused way—but how could it do otherwise? It speaks of the *socialist "essence"* of China's enterprises and of the profit that they make, writing, for example: "It is a glorious responsibility for the socialist enterprises to work hard in order to increase accumulation for the state and make bigger profits. Under socialist conditions what an enterprise gains is, in essence, different from capitalist profit. The gains made by a socialist enterprise are a manifestation of the workers' conscious effort to create material wealth, provide funds for consumption, and accumulate capital for the building of socialism. This differs entirely from capitalist exploitation of the workers' surplus value . . . Improving the management of enterprises and increasing their gains, on the one hand, and the [revisionist] idea of putting profit in command, on the other, are two completely different concepts."

This sort of statement is exactly equivalent to what the Soviet economists say when they, too, speak of "socialist profit" and the "socialist wage"; but it is not enough to stick the adjective "socialist" on an economic category to determine the *social nature* of the reality it refers to. That depends on the *social conditions under which the production process takes place.* Numerous documents of the Cultural Revolution period dealt with this question (even though not always very clearly) and pointed out that one cannot equate state ownership of enterprises with their having a socialist character—the enterprises in question do not possess any socialist "essence" independent of the production relations, the forms of division of labor and of management that prevail in them.

Today, however, the official ideology seeks to deny precisely that which was emphasized during the Cultural Revolution. It is concerned with glorifying profit in order *to call on the workers to "work hard," to be disciplined, and to "obey orders and regulations"*—that is, to cut down the scope of political intervention by the workers. Thus, the editorial of November 9,

1977, in *Jen-min Jih-pao* speaks of the "losses of a political nature" suffered by the enterprises, which must, it says, "be reduced to the minimum."

This fully corresponds to the line which withdraws technological initiative and management from the workers, the revolutionary committees, and the workers' management groups (and also from the various "three-in-one combination" organizations, of which hardly anything is said anymore), in order to concentrate these powers in the hands of the "two chief leaders" in each enterprise. It is clear that this is the current line, as can be seen, for example, in the speech made by Yu Chiu-li at Taching, and in a Radio Peking broadcast of October 18, 1977, which dwelt on the principle by which the "two chief leaders of an enterprise must personally take charge of matters concerned with accumulation and profit."

Whatever phrases may be inserted in order to recall, in ritual fashion, that in the management of enterprises the "class struggle must still be taken as our axis," it is clear that *profit is now to be the central preoccupation.*

This has a number of implications. On the one hand, the stress laid on profit is used to strengthen hierarchical authority, to toughen regulations, and to get rid of intervention by the workers in management matters. On the other hand, the insistence with which the profits to be made by the enterprises is spoken of accompanies an ideological turn. Today practically no mention is made of the distinction between "enterprise profit" (meaning financial profit, the local manifestation of the valorization of capital) and "social profit," the importance of which was stressed at the end of the 1960s and the beginning of the 1970s. Henceforth, therefore, enterprises which do not make a (financial) profit can no longer be singled out as "enterprises of the Taching type," which means that they can no longer be put forward as examples.[6]

The role ascribed to profit is obviously also linked with the *type of industrialization* that is coming to prevail in the name of the "modernization" of industry. (I shall come back to this question.) In any case, historical experience and theory alike teach us that putting the accent on enterprise profit in this way can only aggravate inequalities between regions and hinder the development of local industry and of small- and medium-sized industry. Yet it was this last-mentioned form of development that was characteristic of the mode of industrialization in China (especially after 1958), and it achieved some remarkable successes.

I am not, of course, one of those who think that the line which is dominant in this sphere today is due essentially to "mistakes." More precisely, even if one can speak of "mistakes," it must be seen that these are the result of a *class point of view*, of the tendency to consolidate capitalist relations, capitalist forms of the division of labor, of the organization of production, and of management — and therefore of the tendency to put the role played by the cadres, technicians, and intelligentsia first.

The Struggle Against "Egalitarianism" in the Sphere of Wages

We find the same class line at work in what is being said and done in the sphere of wages. Here the dominant aspect of the present line is the struggle against so-called egalitarianism, and for *differentiation* in wages.

Thus, an article in *Guan-min Jih-pao* of November 1977 goes so far as to say that "egalitarianism is still the biggest problem in China" — this being the actual title of the article. Such an affirmation runs counter to what Mao Tse-tung said in February 1975: "Before Liberation it was more or less like capitalism. Even now we practice an eight-grade wage system, distribution to each in accordance with work done and exchange by means of money, and all this scarcely differs from the old society."

One of the reasons why the accent is now put on the fight against "egalitarianism" is that it is once again a question of resorting to "material incentives" — though, for the moment, this is done with some caution, as the Chinese working class is aware of what that line implies. In practice this takes the form, in a certain number of cases, of going back to piece-wages (whereas, during the Cultural Revolution, piece-wages were replaced by time-wages), and in other, less numerous, cases, the form of more or less generous bonus payments. All this is done in the name of accelerating the growth of the productive forces and increasing the productivity of labor—that is, in the name of arguments of an economistic and productivist character.

One article is especially significant in this connection—the article by Chao Lu-kuan (NCNA, November 22, 1977) which, starting from the principle, "To each according to his work," strives (still with great caution) to make a case for piece-wages (Chao does not mention, of course, Marx's observation that "the piece-wage is the form of wage most appropriate to the capitalist mode of production"[7]) and for "the utilization of the necessary material rewards as a supplementary form."

This article and many like it that have appeared since 1977 increasingly make *individual interest* the driving-force of the struggle for production. This interest is substituted for the role played by a consciousness that one is working to satisfy the people's needs and to build socialism, the role which was put in the forefront during the Cultural Revolution.

Such a substitution corresponds to the interests of the bourgeoisie in the party. It can only *divide the working class* by fostering the growing inequalities among the workers. Going back to piece-wages and material incentives after practicing for years the payment of time-wages, and after having long since renounced material incentives, means taking *an immense step backward*. This step backward favors the managers of enterprises and the technicians: it tends to strengthen the state bourgeoisie, those who occupy leading posts in the economic and administrative machinery and in the party. This is the *class content* of the new line, whatever may be the pretexts invoked by its supporters.

The New Orientations in Agricultural Policy

Since the end of 1976 a new orientation in agricultural matters has become apparent. Basically, this reduces the initiative of the peasant masses and increasingly subordinates them to a highly centralized leadership over which the working people exercise no real control. It tends to impose on the people's communes work norms that are decided externally, and to promote technological changes that are also mainly inspired by organs situated far away from the immediate producers.

The class content of this new orientation is clear. On the one hand, it is a matter of favoring the development of a production process that subordinates the peasant masses, to the utmost degree possible, to domination by the cadres, local and central, and so to a bourgeoisie of a new type. On the other hand (but the two aspects are interconnected), it is a matter of creating conditions enabling the maximum amount of surplus labor to be extracted from the peasantry, so that they may pay the highest possible amount of tribute to finance the "four modernizations" which are indispensable if the power of the state bourgeoisie is to be consolidated.

While the class content of the new orientation in agricultural policy is clear, it is nevertheless true that it takes as its pretext certain real problems whose importance was previously underestimated. These problems are, in the first place, problems of production: after progressing in a remarkable way for about ten years, agricultural production seems to have reached a threshold which it is essential to rise above in order to cope with the food needs of an increasing population.[8] These problems are also problems of consolidating the existing production relations and of changing the process of labor and production, which includes technological change.[9] They are problems, likewise, of the superstructure, of ideology and politics. There can be no question of reviewing all of them here, and even less of claiming that they can be solved in a simple way. It is only possible to examine some of the "solutions" that are being put forward today, and to consider what they imply and what their class meaning is.

Two forms of the tendency for the structures of collective production to break down have been frequently mentioned since the end of 1976, though it is clear that the same phenomena existed earlier, having been mentioned in a number of "big-character posters," especially in South China.

One of these forms is the increase in size of individual plots and in the extent of family activities associated with them. As far back as December 1976, the existence of these problems was mentioned, for example in a broadcast from Radio Nanking on December 13.

Another form of the tendency for collective labor to break down (and one which seems to present a sufficient threat to collective agricultural production for it to have been mentioned often) is the increasing involvement of rural labor in extra-agricultural activities, along with an uncontrolled movement of the work force. These phenomena were condemned, for instance, in a report entitled "Strengthen the Front Line of Agricultural Production," which was circulated by the NCNA on September 2, 1977. This document mentions that certain collective or state production units recruit labor from other communes or brigades. It also mentions that, in some communes and brigades, workers engage in other activities besides agricultural production, and that these communes or brigades include too many unproductive members.

Following the publication of this report, the provincial radio stations mentioned that investigation groups were being formed by the party committees. One of the tasks of these groups is to ensure that temporary or contract workers who are no longer with their communes go back to the countryside.

Here we are certainly faced with serious phenomena which contribute to threatening the continuity and, *a fortiori*, the growth of agricultural production. I know of no fundamental analysis directed at accounting for these phenomena and drawing conclusions from them. On the other hand, we know that since the end of 1976 concrete measures of every kind have been taken, about which I now want to say something, because, as I mentioned earlier, these measures seem to me to have a clear class meaning, even though they are, or may appear to be, to some extent in contradiction one with another.

A first series of measures aims at reducing the size of individual plots, where these exceed the percentage laid down in the regulations. These measures are aimed at consolidating the economy of the people's communes, which is indispensable for increased collective production, but they may correspond either to a revolutionary or to a revisionist orientation; in present conditions the revisionists must also rely upon collective agricultural production adequate to sustain their program of "modernization."

Other measures, mentioned by Radio Peking on December 20, 1976, aim at restricting certain collective "additional productive activities." This seems to imply a threat to rural industrialization, which has developed on a large scale since the Great Leap Forward and the Cultural Revolution. It is essential that it be continued, especially in order to reduce the contradiction between town and country, to ensure a socialist development of the productive forces, and to satisfy the immediate needs of the masses.

To be sure, the restriction on collective "additional productive activities" may seem to be dictated by "problems of labor supply," but this restriction corresponds basically to a revisionist conception—to the desire of the leaders of centralized industry to control *all* industrial production. It is therefore not possible to suppose that its sole or even its main purpose is to ensure that more labor power is available for agricultural production.

This is all the less possible because family or individual subsidiary activities are being encouraged, and rural markets have been made respectable again. I find it hard to estimate whether this is some sort of "concession" granted to the peasants (so as to enable them to increase their incomes), or whether the purpose is to obtain certain additional products which it seems impossible at present to obtain in any other way. In any case, the line of favoring family and individual subsidiary production is very clear. It was confirmed by a national conference held in the autumn of 1977 at which it was declared that wide scope should be allowed to these productive activities, which, it was said, constitute "an essential complement to the socialist economy." It was added that these ought not to be criticized as representing a "form of capitalism," for such criticism would be characteristic of a "revisionist line" (NCNA, October 13, 1977).

More significant still, in my opinion, is the way in which the present political line tries to solve the problems created by the "shortage of labor power" from which Chinese agriculture suffers. The dominant aspect of this line is the resort to authoritarian measures imposed upon the peasantry from above. This is done under the slogan of "rational use of rural labor power." Thus, on November 23, 1976, Radio Haikow (Hainan) said that it is necessary "to learn to organize labor power" and called for the production team to be subjected to the "unified command of the brigade and the commune." It was also said that labor power must be *sent* wherever production can most effectively be increased and wherever it is possible to get the best results.

I do not doubt that the "economic objective" aimed at is desirable. But I very gravely doubt whether the methods advocated are either "socialist" or "effective." Actually, the proposed measures lead to the peasants being treated as a work force which a unified command sends wherever it considers their intervention will be most useful. This is a capitalist, not a socialist, way of organizing labor, a form of organization which the peasants cannot but resist. It is a long time since things were "organized" in this way in the collective farms of the USSR, and everyone knows the result of that!

We know, too, the setbacks which have resulted from attempts to treat the struggle for increasing agricultural production as so many "battles" to be directed, more or less centrally, by "general staffs." Yet a number of recent declarations show that such pseudo-military measures are viewed with favor by the present leadership of the Chinese Communist Party. Adoption of measures of this kind means *a lack of confidence in the peasants.*

This lack of confidence cannot but be reinforced by the way the peasants inevitably, and rightly, react to measures which tend to transform them into a work force required to "maneuver" under the orders of a *"unified command."* As though the Chinese peasants do not *themselves* know how to produce and how to organize so as to increase production! The tendency to organize the peasants' work from above and in an authoritarian way entails unavoidable consequences. The new leadership prepares to confront these consequences with a series of measures announced in a report circulated by NCNA on September 2, 1977. So far as the immediate future is concerned, these measures consist of tightening up labor discipline, laying down a system of work norms, and fixing rates of payment related to these norms. The report states explicitly that it is necessary to strengthen *labor discipline, record attendance at work, strengthen the system of responsibility,* improve the organization of work, establish "simple" methods of payment (related to work done), organize *emulation,* and undertake regular *evaluation* of the work done by individuals and production units.

The summer of 1977 already saw some districts taking this road. On June 16, 1977, Radio Lanchow quoted as an example the district of Hoshui, in Kansu province, which had introduced "a good system of recording attendance at work" and was applying a *system of work norms* combined with a *system of inspection.* This signifies a complete reversal of the line followed since the Cultural Revolution, during which fixed norms were exceptional and a system of *self-evaluation* prevailed.

The Soviet experience has shown fully that these systems of fixing work norms and checking on the peasants' work only bring mediocre or even derisory results.

"Accelerated" Mechanization of Agriculture

The way in which the leadership of the Chinese Communist Party has decided to speed up the mechanization of agriculture shows clearly that this leadership is far from supposing that the methods of work organization which it advocates (but which it is obliged to resort to since it lacks confidence in the peasants) will solve the problems of agricultural production. Indeed, it is one thing to take the correct and necessary decision to follow the road of mechanizing agriculture, and quite another to *rush hastily* along this road as the Chinese Communist Party is doing now, as when it says that mechanization is to be realized "in the main" by 1980. Such haste leads inevitably to disappointment, but it is doubtless dictated by social contradictions, since "technological requirements" would, in fact, dictate a step-by-step, methodical advance.[10]

This haste, and the social contradictions of which it is the product, together with the striving to subject the peasantry to a unified command, seems to be leading to an abandonment of the correct policy, hitherto accepted, of carrying out mechanization principally *on the basis of each brigade and each commune,* with these units relying mainly on their own resources.

Numerous statements make it plain that agricultural equipment is to be centralized in workshops dealing with several brigades and communes (which reminds one of the machine-and-tractor stations in the USSR, which were set up in haste in similar circumstances and for the same reasons, and which have produced disappointing and well-known results). These central workshops are controlled by the party's regional committees. Clearly, the direction taken (which is logical, given the current policy) points toward "great agricultural battles" led by the provincial authorities, who have machinery centers at their disposal and act through the prefectures and municipalities. Everything is to be placed under the command of the party. The party committees are called upon, accordingly, to form "leading groups for agricultural mechanization."

The centralization thus advocated tends to take away from the people's communes and brigades the role they used to play in producing small-scale mechanical equipment appropriate to their needs. This centralization, and the haste with which an operation as serious and difficult as agricultural mechanization is being conducted, are now causing a number of difficulties. The difficulty most talked about is one that is well known in the Soviet Union, namely, the problem of supplying the agricultural sector with *spare parts.*

In this connection, let us dwell for a moment upon three readers' letters published by *Jen-min Jih-pao* on January 6, 1978 (and circulated by NCNA on the same day). One of these letters was sent by a cadre from the people's commune of Hsiehtun (Chouhsien district, Anhwei province) to the Red East Tractor Factory in Loyang. The letter criticizes the factory for not having solved correctly the problem of spare parts. The commune was unable to find the spare parts that it needed anywhere (this was during the winter of 1976). After having written unsuccessfully to the tractor factory, the commune decided to send a delegation, but the delegation was not received. Only after a letter had been sent to the factory through *Jen-min Jih-pao* did the factory "reconsider its attitude" and make a "self-criticism" to the effect that its shortcomings were "principally due to the frenzied sabotage of agricultural mechanization by the 'Gang of Four.'"[11] The management of the factory said that it was determined to "clean up the labor regulations."

The letter from the Hsiehtun people's commune to *Jen-min Jih-pao* then says that after this "self-criticism," the factory sent several technicians to the commune; they examined the tractor and took two of the commune's tractor drivers back with them to the factory to buy the spare parts they needed.[12]

If I have given so much space to an affair that might seem to be no more than an anecdote, it is because it seems to me highly significant in a number of ways:

(1) It shows that already in the winter of 1976, when agricultural mechanization had not gone far, it was very hard for a people's commune to get spare parts for its tractors.

(2) It reveals a situation quite similar to the one that the Soviet Union has known for over forty years.

(3) It allows us to predict the grave risks that China's agriculture will run after mechanization if the factories continue to "deal with" problems of supplying spare parts in this way.

(4) It shows that the basic cause of these problems was not even touched upon, since the management of the factory got out of its awkward spot by blaming its shortcomings on the influence of the "Gang of Four" and took the opportunity to "clean up the labor regulations," that is, to tighten labor dis-

cipline, whereas what was needed was to solve a problem of priorities in production, the management of stock, and distribution.

To anyone with any experience of the problems presented by the mechanization of agriculture, it is obvious that the current "acceleration" signifies a *flight forward* caused by the aggravation of social contradictions.[13] These are bound up with the way in which an attempt is being made to *command* the peasantry—that is, with the development of bourgeois relations and practices. In its turn, this development bears witness to the changes that have taken place in the relations of strength between classes. These changes are increasingly leading to a situation in which a massive introduction of modern technology is seen as the way to solve all difficulties. The haste with which the Chinese Communist Party is trying to carry out the "four modernizations" is typical of the present situation.

The acceleration of the mechanization of agriculture and the emphasis on the "four modernizations" reflect a bourgeois conception of *technological progress*.[14] In this way, a process is beginning that inevitably must result in raising, substantially and rapidly, the *rate of accumulation*, which must tell heavily upon the standard of living and working conditions of the workers and peasants.

It is also important that the *priority* assigned to mechanization over other technological changes in agriculture testifies to the class nature of the present political line. Actually, it is *not* mechanization alone that will make it possible to solve the problem of increasing agricultural production (which does not mean that mechanization is not *one element in the solution* to this problem). The problem can be solved only through *differentiated methods*—by developing the use of selected seeds, by diversifying the fertilizers used[15]—which presupposes *mass experimentation and initiative*. But the current line does not point that way. It points toward the increased subordination of the peasants to a central authority which will be in a position to extort the maximum of surplus labor from them. Mechanization is seen mainly as a *means of more effectively ensuring this subordination*, by favoring the predominance of dead labor (centrally controlled) over living labor.

The Purging of the Leading Organs in Agriculture

It is in this context that the way in which the task of "carrying through the revolution in the superstructure" is now interpreted acquires its full meaning. Thus, in *Hung Chi* (no. 6, 1977), Wang Chien defines this task as one of "strengthening the revolutionization of the leading organs" by ensuring that the leadership is in the hands of "Marxists," and of "educating the peasants in Marxism, Leninism, and Mao Tse-tung Thought."

To those who can read, this means *purging the organs of leadership*, removing all who do not share the present views on discipline, command, "modernization," and so on. It also means "educating the peasants" by inculcating in them these present views, *but no longer learning from them*.

Foreign Trade Policy

The current orientation of economic policy includes many other aspects which reveal its revisionist character. They cannot all be examined here, but something must be said about certain problems of foreign trade and about the way it is proposed that these be "solved." A particularly significant document in this connection was presented at one of the conferences held in early 1977 on Mao's work *On the Ten Major Relationships*, namely, the sixteenth in the series, which was devoted to foreign trade.

This document (broadcast on February 15, 1977, by Radio Peking) sets forth the concept of "normal foreign trade" (which has nothing in common with Marxism, and which is, more precisely, anti-Marxist). This concept aims at "justifying" the priority given to increased exports of coal and oil in exchange for imports of new technology and equipment, thus seeking to find "arguments" in support of a policy which would give

China's foreign trade a structure similar, as Chang Chun-chiao correctly observed, to that of a "colonial economy."

I do not, of course, mean that this is the "aim" pursued by the present leadership of the Chinese Communist Party. They certainly want to modernize China and make it independent of the big imperialist powers. What I do mean is that, by utilizing the bourgeois notion of "normal foreign trade" and giving priority to exports of raw materials, *this leadership is incapable of attaining the goal it does aim at.* The Soviet Union, which took the same road nearly fifty years ago, is still, in its relations with the industrial countries, mainly an exporter of raw materials. It has not succeeded in developing technologies that would put it on the same footing as the industrialized countries, and so continues to import technology and equipment on a mass scale.

The situation in which the Soviet Union finds itself is not, of course, due mainly to a particular "conception" of foreign trade, but this "conception" forms *part of a whole*, of a *political line* which has led to this result. I think, too, for the reasons I have set out above and for others which I shall set out later, that it is fundamentally the *same* political line that is triumphant in China today. This is a *revisionist line*—a line which, with certain special features, was applied in the Soviet Union in the 1930s.[16]

Incidentally, I note that the empty notion of "normal foreign trade" *is not an isolated case.* Official documents in China increasingly use such expressions, which are quite alien to Marxism.

The Destruction of the Reform of Education

But let us return to other concrete manifestations of the *offensive* now being conducted against the Cultural Revolution. One of the most important of these concerns the *system of education.* When it is said (as in the circular of the Central Committee of the Chinese Communist Party on holding a national science conference, September 18, 1977; see *Peking Review*, no. 40, 1977) that "we must do a really good job in the educational revolution," while at the same time *the end of the Cultural Revolution has been proclaimed*, this can only be interpreted to mean that it is intended to carry through to completion *the counter-revolution in education*, that is, to reject most of the changes accomplished since 1966. A study of recent decisions and documents proves that this is what is happening and that, here too, we observe a "leap backward."

The recruitment of students is once more being effected on an *elitist* basis. Examinations have been restored to a place of honor (see *Cahiers de la Chine Nouvelle*, no. 2748, 1977), and give an advantage to those with academic and book knowledge. Thus, *Jen-min Jih-pao* of October 21, 1977, while acknowledging that some manual workers with practical experience may be admitted to the universities, stresses that it is necessary "to take those who are the best on the intellectual plane" and that "the students must be selected, in a given proportion, from among the new graduates of the second-cycle secondary school." This means a partial return to the system that existed before the Cultural Revolution, beginning with the abolition of the two-to-three-year probationary periods that future intellectuals and cadres have to spend in the country. It means also abandoning the designation of those who are to go to university by their fellow-workers. In fact, in October 1977 between 20 and 30 percent of the students were recruited directly from among the "best" pupils of the secondary schools. The information available to me shows that, as was to be expected, these are largely the *children of cadres*, who have in many cases been *specially prepared for these examinations* by means of cramming. The privileges possessed by those who have money, and, above all, by the sons and daughters of cadres, are thus reinforced.

The lengthy eulogy to the situation *before* the Cultural Revolution which we find in the circular of September 18, 1977, shows clearly that the present leadership of the Chinese Communist Party wishes to return to a similar situation.

Equally characteristic is the reconstitution of a *dual network of educational institutions*, which was severely condemned during the Cultural Revolution. As *Jen-min Jih-pao* of October

26, 1977, explains: "Admission to colleges is still limited. The young people who fail their examinations are the majority. So long as they continue to study diligently and strive to master scientific and cultural knowledge, they will have a second chance to take the examination in the future, or else they will be able to pursue advanced studies in the July 21 Worker Colleges and other part-time universities." Thus the "best" will go directly into higher education while the rest will swell the ranks of the skilled manual workers.

I do not claim that everything that was done in the sphere of education during the Cultural Revolution was "perfect" or not in need of serious discussion. On the contrary—and this seems to me inevitable—I think, based on what has been said by students and teachers who have been to China during recent years, that certain aspects of the reforms introduced left something to be desired, and that substantial improvements were called for. But it seems clear to me that *it is not by going back to the situation before the Cultural Revolution that improvements can be made.* Instead, there should be an extensive public assessment of the lessons to be drawn from the experience of the Cultural Revolution in the sphere of education, and this requires a broad debate. But this is not what is done when a return is made to 1965, while declaring that "we must do a really good job in the educational revolution."

This way of behaving is, moreover, in line with the hastiness characteristic of the whole of the current campaign for the "four modernizations." Above all, though, it is aimed at *reestablishing the power of the academic authorities, at strengthening the power of the intellectuals and the cadres.* In this respect, the importance being given to mathematics is quite symptomatic, for the same tendency is also developing in Western Europe and in the United States. This importance emerges from numerous articles—for instance, the formulation used by Wu Wen-chiu in *Jen-min Jih-pao* of August 11, 1977: "The degree of a country's industrialization is mainly in direct proportion to the development of mathematics in that country."

This is a baseless assertion aimed at increasing the "prestige" of mathematical knowledge and of those who "possess" it. It forms part of an ideology which emphasizes the role of the intellectuals. It goes far beyond what needs to be said and done in order to restore professional and theoretical knowledge to its proper place, a place which had, without doubt, been lost to some extent during the previous years.

Altogether, the orientation adopted regarding labor discipline and labor regulations, the revolutionary committees in the factories, wage differentials, the organization of agricultural production, the acceleration of agricultural mechanization, the reform of teaching, etc., all form part of the *rejection of the "socialist innovations" contributed by the Cultural Revolution, that is, of the conquests of that revolution.*

We are thus not watching a movement to rectify the mistakes made in the course of the Cultural Revolution—the most important revolutionary movement of the second half of the twentieth century. What we see is an attempt at the theoretical and practical liquidation of this revolutionary movement.

The Attempt to Liquidate the Cultural Revolution "Theoretically"

On the theoretical plane, the leadership of the Chinese Communist Party does not dare to launch a frontal attack on the Cultural Revolution, because this would mean *openly* attacking the line of Mao Tse-tung. It claims to be faithful to this line, because it needs such a claim in order to appear "legitimate." Nevertheless, the present leadership is developing *camouflaged attacks* which are attempts at theoretical "liquidation." The forms assumed by these attacks are many. I shall mention only a few.

One of the most significant consists in *denying the line of demarcation* which the Cultural Revolution represented in the practice and theory of the Chinese Communist Party. We know that Mao Tse-tung regarded this line of demarcation as fundamental. Towards the end of his life, he declared that he had devoted himself to two purposes: "Driving Japanese imperialism out of China and overthrowing Chiang Kai-shek, on the one hand, and, on the other, carrying through the Great Proletarian Cultural Revolution." Mao thus put the Cultural Revolution and the liberation of the country on the same footing.

The present leadership, however, is trying to wipe out the line of demarcation traced by the Cultural Revolution. It is trying to do this not only practically, by its concrete policy and by returning Rightists to posts of command they were removed from between 1966 and 1976, but also "theoretically." It is doing this by gradually ceasing to speak of the "socialist innovations" which came out of the Cultural Revolution. It is doing it by putting formally "on the same level" that which was accomplished between 1949 and 1965 and that which was accomplished between 1966 and 1976, and giving *preference*, de facto, to the conceptions and practices of the earlier period. It thereby denies that, down to 1966, the political line included elements which hindered the march toward socialism, and that, *after 1966, the political line included new revolutionary orientations which implied a radical qualitative change, the transition to a new stage of the revolution.*

This wiping-out of a fundamental line of demarcation is effected by means of a *one-sided* glorification of what was accomplished between 1949 and 1966. It is effected also by attacking the Four and blaming them for having stressed the quite different political significance of the changes which were made then and the changes made in subsequent years. In this connection, the Four are attacked in these terms: "The Gang of Four drew a somber picture of new China during the first seventeen years after its foundation. The Gang did not merely deny that there were any socialist innovations before the Cultural Revolution; they also demanded action against what had been done in the years before the Cultural Revolution in terms of developing socialist innovations, thereby totally repudiating what was realized during the seventeen years following the foundation of the People's Republic of China."

The same document, which was broadcast by Radio Peking on April 8, 1977, stated: "In the seventeen years after the foundation of the People's Republic of China, despite the interference and sabotage constituted by the revisionist line of Liu Shao-chi, the revolutionary line of Chairman Mao always remained in the leading position."

The aim of this statement is not merely to attack the Four. It is also an underestimation of the "interference" from the revisionist line during the years 1949-65. It is vital for the present leadership to do this, because it is returning to a revisionist line itself.[17] It means, further, denying the fundamental difference between the revolutionary line of before and after 1966. This difference relates to the movement of the revolution into a *new stage*—a stage that the present leadership wishes to hear no more about.

We find the same desire to wipe out this fundamental line of demarcation in the circular, already quoted, of September 18, 1977, which blames the Four for having "negated the fact that Chairman Mao's revolutionary line has occupied the dominant position in this field [i.e., science and technology] since the foundation of New China" (*Peking Review*, no. 40, 1977). Yet a formulation like this obscures the situation which existed between 1949 and 1965, the situation that made the Cultural Revolution necessary.

As I mentioned earlier, the attempt to liquidate the Cultural Revolution "theoretically" takes many forms and gives rise to varied formulations. Here are some that are especially significant.

For example, whereas during the Cultural Revolution it was said that every enterprise was a place where the class struggle went on and that production itself was pursued amid definite class relations and class contradictions, it is now said that an enterprise is above all *a place of production*, interpreting in a one-sided way and isolating from its context a phrase of Mao Tse-tung's. This same theme was taken up in April 1977 by Sung Chen-ming, secretary of the party committee at Taching, who went so far as to say: "Throughout the world, production is the principal concern of every factory, every country, and every nation." This is a formula which all the capitalists of the world repeat *ad nauseam*.

In a different form, the same theme was expounded by the Chinese press in November 1977, when a series of documents were published which *separated in mechanical fashion* the class struggle from the struggle for production, thereby denying that these struggles are interconnected, and that the former basically dominates the latter. Thus, it was stated that "Revolution is the struggle of one class against another and aims at altering social relations between men; production is the struggle of man against nature. The laws governing production differ from the laws governing the class struggle" (document broadcast by Radio Peking on November 27, 1977).

This formulation is completely silent about the fact that the "struggle against nature" always develops under *definite social conditions*, within *definite class relations*, and that *the way it is carried on also involves class consequences.* Marx explained all that long ago, and the Cultural Revolution drew the *political deductions* from it. Today, however, the leaders are trying to make people forget it so that they can practice the most vulgar "economism."

This economism can be seen in Wang Chien's article in *Hung Chi* (no. 6, 1977), in which he defends the idea that a change in the production relations and in the superstructure in present-day China must be governed by the requirements of the "development of the productive forces," so as to "strengthen the material basis for consolidating the dictatorship of the proletariat." Here we find ourselves back with the theme of the *primacy of the development of the productive forces,* a theme rightly denounced during the Cultural Revolution and one which served the Soviet state bourgeoisie as an ideological weapon for extending and consolidating its power.

In reality, this theme dominates the whole series of sixteen conferences held on the pretext of discussing *On the Ten Major Relationships.* This becomes apparent when we examine *Hung Chi* (no. 1, 1977). There is nothing here about the necessity for revolutionary transformation of production relations, though this transformation is the fundamental objective of the uninterrupted revolution under the dictatorship of the proletariat. All that is discussed is "adjusting those parts of production relations" that hinder the development of the productive forces, because, we are told, the "aim of the socialist revolution is to emancipate the productive forces."

We come back, here as well, to an economism which makes the productive forces, and not the class struggle, the fundamental revolutionary factor, so that this sort of statement can appear: "In the last analysis, the economic basis is the decisive factor in social progress, and the productive forces are the most active and revolutionary factor in the economic basis. Thus, in the last analysis, it is the productive forces that determine production relations" (NCNA, September 21, 1977).

Thus the theses maintained by Liu Shao-chi at the Eighth Party Congress in 1956 reappear—theses which, though still condemned in words, are now being reiterated without acknowledgment.

Back to the Theme
That a "Socialist System" Exists

In order to provide a theoretical "foundation" for its economism and productivism, and to oppose any radical change in production relations (and so in the division of labor, in the privileges of the cadres and technicians, etc.), the new leadership of the Chinese Communist Party returns to other old themes which the Cultural Revolution had made it possible to criticize. One of these was that of the "socialist system," a concept which tended to replace the concept of the *transition to socialism* and which fulfills the same function as that of the "socialist mode of production" in the ideology of the Stalin period and in Soviet revisionism.

The commentaries devoted to the sixteen conferences that discussed *On the Ten Major Relationships* speak of the "socialist system" which was allegedly "established" in 1956 and which has now to be consolidated by developing the productive forces.

At the heart of the concept of the "socialist system" we find the concept of "socialist ownership," which is itself identified with state ownership. These *identifications* signify that recognition is no longer given to the existence of a series of *contradictions*, although this is in fact one of the main contributions of *On the Ten Major Relationships*, and that, even in the event that this is recognized, *primacy* is accorded to *unity over contradiction*.

The seventh of the conferences declared: "Since the factories are owned by the state, the relation between the factories and the workers has, to some extent, been embodied in the relation between the state and the workers." The purpose of this "theoretical" rubbish is to claim that, since the workers are "masters of the state" and the state is "master of the factories," the workers are therefore "masters of the factories."

In this way the contradictions of the transition to socialism (including those which were pointed out by Lenin in 1921) are simply denied. The workers have only to *obey the orders* they are given, for these orders are given them by themselves! A splendid dialectic, aimed at defending the interests of a state bourgeoisie!

The same fundamental role attributed to "socialist ownership," or "public ownership," is proclaimed in many other writings. For example, when the emulation campaigns were launched, *Jen-min Jih-pao* of March 10, 1977, stated calmly that "under socialism the working people are the masters of society, and the relations within this society are relations of cooperation between comrades."

The existence of the bourgeoisie is ignored and, of course, there is no question of recognizing its presence in the party and at the head of many enterprises. Thus some basic themes of the Cultural Revolution are repudiated.

The typically revisionist refusal to recognize the existence of the fundamental contradiction between bourgeoisie and proletariat also enables Chi Chen to write in *Hung Chi* (no. 3, 1977): "In the socialist enterprises the working class is master. The basic interests of the workers, the cadres, and the technicians are identical. Their relations are relations of mutual aid and cooperation between comrades. At the same time, owing to the division of labor, differences continue to exist between manual work and mental work, and some contradictions survive. These are contradictions among the people." In this way the class struggle is denied, together with the decisive importance of the struggle to overcome the contradiction between manual and mental work.

But it is not so easy to wipe out the teachings of the ten years of the Cultural Revolution. In particular, it is not easy to make people forget what was said during those years, especially by Chang Chun-chiao, who made a frontal attack (even if not always with sufficient clarity) on some of the problems presented by so-called socialist ownership. Certain "theoreticians" cannot avoid, therefore, recalling (while distorting so as to make criticism easier) some of Chang's statements. An example is provided by the article in *Hung Chi* (no. 5, 1977) in which Lin Chin-jan attacks the observations made by Chang Chunchiao in a piece published in 1975 under the title: "Complete Dictatorship over the Bourgeoisie." We know that in this piece Chang sought to determine the nature of the *limits* to the socialist transformation of ownership in China, limits indicated by the current formulation stating that this transformation has been accomplished "in the main." By analyzing this problem Chang took an important step forward, for he stressed the juridical and formal aspects of this transformation. He showed the need for a revolutionary change in *production relations*, thereby epitomizing one of the central aims of the Cultural Revolution.[18]

It is precisely this central aim of the Cultural Revolution, together with the theoretical formulations corresponding to it, that Lin Chin-jan attacks in his article. In order to make his attack convincing, Lin Chin-jan speaks of the "fundamental" completion of the socialist transformation of ownership and declares that, as a result of this "fundamental" completion, the class struggle has to develop mainly on the ideological and political fronts. Lin Chin-jan thus deletes *that which is decisive, namely, the struggle waged by the workers themselves with a view to transforming the labor process and production and, thereby, production relations*. He advocates substituting for the class struggle as this developed during the Cultural Revolution (a struggle concerned with the different forms of the social division of labor) a "struggle of ideas," a struggle between "modern ideology" and the vestiges of "old" ideas. This abandonment of the class struggle implies the transformation of Marxism into its opposite. It enables the state bourgeoisie to attack demands which workers may advance, on the grounds that these are "incompatible with the development of the productive forces," and are due to the fact that these workers are still subject to the influence of "bourgeois and petty-bourgeois ideas."

Lin Chin-jan's article continues as might be expected from the economistic nature of this thesis. From his conception of a "fundamental" socialist change of ownership, he concludes that the principal aspect of the continuation of the revolution under the dictatorship of the proletariat consists in developing a "powerful material basis." All this amounts to is substituting the struggle for production for the struggle between the proletariat and the bourgeoisie, and calling for the struggle for production to be led by experts and technicians. By following this road one can only strengthen the capitalist division of labor and those capitalist production relations which have not yet been destroyed.

It seems that many Chinese workers and party cadres are not letting themselves be misled by these revisionist and economistic conceptions. The ideologists in the service of the present leadership therefore keep on returning to the problems raised by Chang Chun-chiao's article. An example is the article by Wang Hui-teh (*Peking Review*, no. 1, 1978) entitled: "Why Did Chang Chun-chiao Kick Up a Fuss over the Question of Ownership?" In this article Wang Hui-teh blames Chang Chun-chiao for repeating in 1975 a phrase uttered by Mao in April 1969, when he said: "It seems that it won't do not to carry out the Great Proletarian Cultural Revolution, for our foundation is not solid. Judging from my observations, I am afraid that in a fairly large majority of factories—I don't mean all or the overwhelming majority of them—leadership was not in the hands of genuine Marxists and the masses of workers."

According to Wang there is no longer any need for concern with the problem of management of the enterprises, for, thanks to the Cultural Revolution, "only the leadership in a very small number of factories was not in the hands of the proletariat," so that, since power is also held by the working class, the problem of socialist ownership has been "resolved."

Wang's argument raises a series of questions. First, the question of the managerial personnel of the state enterprises. This question is explicitly mentioned by Wang, who declares that, thanks to the Cultural Revolution, it has been definitively settled in favor of socialism. But whence does Wang derive this "certainty"? Between 1969 and 1975, and, *a fortiori*, between 1976 and 1978, have not many things happened, in particular the return *en masse* of the right-wingers who had been eliminated by the Cultural Revolution? Do we not have grounds for supposing that the situation today is *worse* than in 1969?

Finally, the problem of socialist ownership is also that of the class nature of state power. Chang Chun-chiao tried to deal with this problem dialectically (I do not claim that he entirely succeeded) by showing that the class nature of power is not fixed once and for all, that it is determined by the class struggle between the proletariat and the bourgeoisie, a struggle which goes on within the party, so that power is never "purely proletarian" but can pass into the hands of the state bourgeoisie (something that Mao also said when he declared that the Chinese Communist Party could, in certain circumstances, develop into a "fascist party"). But Wang declines, and with reason, to discuss these problems in that way. For him the questions of power and of ownership have been "solved," and he claims to "prove" this by resorting, tautologically, to quotations, which, moreover, he interprets in his own fashion. This method produces the following "reasoning": "First, 'China is a socialist country.' That is to say, our society is socialist in nature, not capitalist. Secondly, as for the economic base of our society, the system of ownership has already been changed from feudal, capitalist, and small-production private ownership into socialist public ownership. Thirdly, we must see to it that the supreme leadership of the party and state will not fall into the hands of bourgeois conspirators and careerists like Lin Piao.

Ours is a state under the dictatorship of the proletariat. . . ."

What we have here is a series of assertions, not a demonstration. The first two assertions assume that the question has been settled. The last leaves absolutely open the "socialist ownership" question of what elements of bourgeois domination existed in 1975, and in what way the dictatorship of the proletariat was combined with its opposite, and the question of whether or not the class nature of the state was changed after the events of October 1976 and the installation in power of the group led by Hua Kuo-feng and Teng Hsiao-ping.

The problem of the nature of property relations and forms of appropriation cannot be solved except by *concrete analyses* of all the matters mentioned above. This is what Chang Chun-chiao was trying to do in his article, and what the ideologists of the present leadership cannot accept. For them there is no problem—state ownership is "socialist" and the workers have only to "work hard" and "obey orders" in order to strengthen and extend this ownership. It is a thesis which negates the teachings of the Cultural Revolution and which serves the interests of the state bourgeoisie.

One thing more about this question, so as to emphasize how dominant is a purely juridical (which means *anti-Marxist*) conception of "socialist ownership." An example of this dominance is provided by the series of articles by Hsueh Mu-chiao published in *Peking Review* (nos. 49-52, 1977), in which he goes so far as to say that in 1953 it was enough for the state to transform some private capitalist enterprises into mixed enterprises, by investing capital in them, taking charge of supplying them with raw materials and marketing their products, and sending in someone to manage them, for these enterprises to become " 'three-fourths' socialist" (*Peking Review*, no. 52, 1977). This is an absolute caricature of Marxism, and illustrates very well the nature of the "Marxism" practiced by the present leadership of the Chinese Communist Party.

The Relations Between Agriculture and Industry, and Between Heavy and Light Industry

The same abandonment of Marxism in favor of a caricature

of Marxism is shown in connection with the relations between agriculture and industry, and between heavy and light industry. It proceeds in an extremely confused way owing to the *formal* "fidelity" proclaimed by the present leadership of the Chinese Communist Party to the political line of Mao Tsetung, a "fidelity" which contradicts its actual practice.

The result is more or less as follows (shown, for instance, by the report of the third conference devoted to *On the Ten Major Relationships*, which was broadcast by Radio Shanghai on February 10, 1977). On the one hand, the priorities accepted by the Chinese Communist Party under Mao's leadership are reaffirmed, in this order: agriculture, light industry, heavy industry. On the other hand, emphasis is placed on the "objective economic law of priority growth of the means of production" (which is, in fact, a law of capitalist development), whereas the *development of agriculture is seen mainly from the standpoint of its contribution to the accumulation of capital*. These points were repeated and accentuated in the report of the fourth conference (Radio Peking, February 3, 1977), devoted to the Soviet path of industrialization. This path is praised, with criticism confined to the "one-sided" character of the priority given to heavy industry at the expense of agriculture. Completely neglected is the problem of equilibrium in exchange between agricultural and industrial products.

In short, here too we come back to an economistic and productivistic conception which is the "theoretical" expression of the present line. In this domain there is a return *not merely to what prevailed before the Cultural Revolution, but even to conceptions that prevailed in China as far back as 1956.*

The "Pace" of Development

On the plane of class relations this backsliding is linked with the strengthening of the positions of the intelligentsia, the cadres, and the specialists, that is, of the state bourgeoisie (I shall endeavor later on to inquire into the conditions which have made this strengthening possible). This strengthening is reflected in the ever greater importance accorded to the "pace" of development.

This question is at the heart of the preoccupations of the present leadership. Significantly, the central organs of the Chinese press made it the principal theme of their joint editorial published on New Year's Day 1978. Here were phrases such as the following which had disappeared from the Chinese press after the Cultural Revolution: "The speed of construction is not just an economic question, it is a serious political question. Why do we say the socialist system is superior? In the final analysis, it is because the socialist system can create higher labor productivity and make the national economy develop faster than capitalism. . . . The question at present is that we must advance at high speed instead of resting content with what we have achieved. . . . In a word, quickening the pace of economic construction is dictated by the development of international and domestic class struggles" (*Peking Review*, no. 1, 1978).

Thus, *acceleration* of the "pace of development" is supposed to be "deduced" from the requirements of the class struggle, whereas, in fact, it is a matter of trying to *substitute the struggle for production for the workers' class struggle*, that is, *to subject the workers to the "requirements" of rates of production, to demand of them more and more work and discipline.*

The stress thus laid upon the pace of production has a dual meaning on the plane of class relations. On the one hand, as I have said, it reflects the strengthening of the position of the intelligentsia, the cadres, and the specialists. On the other, it is a *means of contributing to a further strengthening of these positions*—not only by subjecting the workers and peasants to increasingly severe labor discipline and work norms, but also by making the leading role assumed by the intelligentsia and the specialists seem a *necessity*. In this respect the editorial quoted is very significant, for it accords central importance to the intellectuals, to education, and to the acquisition of scientific knowledge. In this way *the stress laid upon speeding up the pace of development also serves as an argument for attacking the reform of education carried out during the Cultural Revolution.*

On the plane of production relations, the stress laid on

speeding up the pace implies, since it is linked not with revolutionizing the production relations but with the increased role of "science" concentrated in the hands of "specialists," an *increasing dominance* of capitalist expanded reproduction, and so a *growth in the rate of accumulation* and in the demands of *self-valorization of capital*. It therefore implies *submission of the workers to the demands of profit*. Along the *capitalist road* which is thus being followed one necessarily comes up against the *actual limits of capitalist accumulation*, and this leads inevitably to *economic crises* which have grave repercussions on the standard of living of the masses and on the subsequent scope of the development of the productive forces.

Soviet experience shows that, though these crises develop under specific conditions, they are nonetheless real. I have no room here to deal fundamentally with this problem, which I shall examine in detail in the third volume of *Class Struggles in the USSR*. The stress on speeding-up the pace calls for some further observations. In the first place, it is of the same order as the productivist slogan issued by Stalin in the 1930s: "Tempos decide everything." The application of this slogan led to the grave crises of 1932-33 and 1936-37, which were accompanied by unprecedented *political convulsions* and, after 1938, by a *fundamental change in recruitment to the party*, which became very largely a recruitment from the intelligentsia, a recruitment of cadres, technicians, and specialists.

In the second place, the present leadership justifies its productivist line not only by invoking the alleged requirement that the "socialist order" must realize "rates of development higher than those of capitalism," but also the alleged necessity to "put an end to the protracted stagnation and even regression in the country's economy," said to be due to the doings of the Four. This "argument" is a flagrant falsehood. *There has been no protracted stagnation or regression in the country's economy.* Between 1965, the last year before the Cultural Revolution, and the most recent years for which we have estimates, there was no stagnation. Production of electric power increased from 42 to 108 billion kwh (in 1974), production of steel from 12.5 to 32.8 million tons (in 1974), of coal from 220 to 389 million tons (in 1974), and of oil from 10.8 to between 75 and 80 million tons (in 1975).[19] To speak of a *protracted* period of stagnation, and even of regression, is in complete conflict with reality, and is aimed merely at slandering the Cultural Revolution itself.

The increase in production has been even greater where production of machinery is concerned. The overall index for this branch of production, taking 100 = 1957 as the base year, rose from 257 in 1965 to 1,156 in 1975. These figures are taken from a source so unfriendly as the CIA's handbook![20]

In 1975-76, to be sure, difficulties arose, but these were in the main *political difficulties*, connected with the acute struggle between the revolutionary line and the revisionist line of Teng Hsiao-ping. In the second half of 1976 there were also difficulties arising from the Tangshan earthquake. Thus attributing the problems which appeared then to "interference and sabotage by the Gang of Four" completely distorts the facts. Actually, the Four never "controlled" the economy, and if there was "sabotage" it may be suspected that responsibility for this lies with those who *were* in charge of production — either because they wanted to be able to blame the Four for their own misdeeds, or because their treatment of the workers provoked various manifestations of discontent, including strikes, which the Four may well have supported. In any case, it is a typically bourgeois line of thought to declare that, when strikes occur, responsibility for them lies with "agitators."

Even with the difficulties mentioned above, the available information for 1976 does not show any signs of "protracted stagnation" or "regression." Thus in 1975, production of coal was estimated at 430 million tons, while in 1976 production of oil increased by 13 percent, and production of natural gas increased by 11 percent. During the first quarter of 1976 overall industrial production was 13.4 percent more than in the same period of 1975, and during the first half of 1976 it was 7 percent more than in the same period in 1975.[21] So far as I know, there are no figures available for the second half of 1976.

It may be that, because of the events of 1976, some branches of production may *momentarily* have declined, but that does not signify a protracted period of stagnation or regression.

The foregoing remarks do not in the least imply that *a certain acceleration of pace is not desirable and possible*, but *this acceleration will not be lasting if the basic lines of the Cultural Revolution are abandoned* and the class struggle reduced completely to the struggle for production.

Actually, this reduction amounts to the enslavement of the working people for the purposes of a bourgeoisie striving to increase profit. It implies a renunciation of the workers' class struggle for the revolutionary change of production relations and of social relations as a whole.

The Revisionist Ideology of the Neutrality of Science and Technology

The effects of turning Marxism into its opposite, which is characteristic of the ideology of the present leadership of the Chinese Communist Party, can of course, be observed in all spheres. There is one sphere, though, that I must specially mention — that of science and technology. Here the ideology of the opponents of the Cultural Revolution is marked by its presentation of science and technology as socially "neutral." They thus deny that the way in which science and technology develop depends on the predominant class relations, and that the application of different techniques involves *definite class effects*. This is obviously the case with the forms of technology developed in the imperialist countries. As a rule, they cannot be purely and simply "taken over" in order to serve development along the socialist road: they, too, need to be transformed. This point of view was widely present during the Cultural Revolution. Today it is being forgotten.

The extreme point in this denial of the class determination of techniques occurs where "management techniques" are concerned. For example, *Jen-min Jih-pao* of March 22, 1977, criticized the formulation according to which, in management, one needs to pay attention to three aspects — "the line, the leadership, and mutual relations." It criticized this formulation because it makes no mention of "the most important question, that of developing the productive forces." The question of developing the productive forces is indeed important, but to say that it is the *most* important means *giving it precedence over class relations*, and so taking up a productivist position.

It must be noted, moreover, that the yardstick of "scientificness" occupies a central place in the attempt being made by the present ideologists to eliminate the essential question of class relations. Thus, this same article in *Jen-min Jih-pao* emphasizes that "it is necessary to have a scientific attitude in the managing of modern enterprises. . . . In the managing of modern enterprises it is necessary to employ a number of scientific methods."

The statement reporting the fifteenth conference devoted to *On the Ten Major Relationships* (Radio Peking, February 14, 1977) goes so far as to declare that it is necessary to keep that which is "scientific" in the "advanced techniques of the capitalist countries" in the matter of the "management of enterprises." This formulation presupposes that capitalist management belongs to the sphere of "universal" science and *that the working class can manage production units in the same way as capitalist enterprises are managed.*

Let it be noted that the *Jen-min Jih-pao* document refers to a "quotation" from *On the Ten Major Relationships* which is more than dubious, being obviously falsified and adapted to "current taste." In the version of *On the Ten Major Relationships* which is now officially circulated, we read the following sentences, which in a number of ways fails to correspond either to Mao's style or to the manner in which he deals with problems: "We must firmly reject and criticize all the decadent bourgeois systems, ideologies, and ways of life of foreign countries. But this should in no way prevent us from learning the advance sciences and technologies of capitalist countries and whatever is scientific in the management of their enterprises."

In the version of *On the Ten Major Relationships* which was circulated by the Red Guards during the Cultural Revolution, Mao said nothing like this. This version contained no stereotyped formula about "decadent bourgeois ideologies," and said *nothing about the "scientific" character of the management of enterprises in the capitalist countries.* Mao Tse-tung spoke much more simply.[22] Clearly, Mao Tse-tung's words have been tampered with so as to "justify" the resort to capitalist methods of management by covering this with his authority. The present leadership of the Chinese Communist Party is here taking the same road as those Soviet revisionists who are "learning management" in business schools in the United States.

This "modification" of one of Mao Tse-tung's writings is not an isolated case; this is a regular practice of the new leadership. As another example, in the current version of *On the Ten Major Relationships* a phrase has been introduced which did not appear in previous versions, a phrase which emphasizes the need for strong centralism, *running counter to Mao's emphasis upon decentralization.* The phrase in question runs as follows: "To build a powerful socialist country it is imperative to have a strong and unified central leadership . . ." (*Peking Review*, no. 1, 1977).

In general, what is characteristic of the ideology accepted to-day by the leadership of the Chinese Communist Party and in conflict with the theses of Mao Tse-tung developed during the Cultural Revolution, is its tendency to present science and technology as "neutral," like the productive forces. The idea that there is both a *socialist* and a *capitalist* development of the productive forces, and that only the former promotes control by the workers over the means of production, has completely disappeared. Now there is only general talk about "development of the productive forces." This is closely linked with the thesis according to which, as soon as the "socialist system" exists, everything that develops its "material basis" must strengthen "socialism."

Dogmatism and Revisionism

One might go on examining the ideological themes which the present leadership uses to justify its resort to revisionist practices, practices which no longer have anything in common with the Cultural Revolution. However, I do not think this is necessary, since what has been said is conclusive enough. I wish therefore to end this section of my letter by simply saying that *what characterizes present-day Chinese revisionism is its combination of narrowly empiricist practices and an ideology dominated by dogmatism.*

This dogmatism is shown by the fact that *instead of carrying out a concrete analysis* of social and political realities, the revisionists *proceed by means of assertions and by using quotations from the "classics" of Marxism and from Mao Tse-tung, isolated from their context* (and even, as we have seen, sometimes distorted or invented). Moreover, *no account is taken of the development of the theoretical conceptions of the thinkers quoted.* Thus passages from Mao Tse-tung dating from before the Cultural Revolution are put on the same footing as passages from the Cultural Revolution period. Or, more precisely, *the older quotations are given precedence over the more recent ones.* This does not happen by accident, of course: the more recent passages are rich with an entire experience of struggle against the bourgeoisie in the party, an experience which is highly embarrassing for the present leadership.

Finally, the dogmatism of the period which opened at the end of 1976 is marked by a desire to present fundamental theoretical problems as having been "solved," with a view to preventing further progress in analyses along the line opened up since the Cultural Revolution. In this connection it is highly significant that it has been stated that Mao "created the complete and masterly theory of the continuation of the revolution under the dictatorship of the proletariat" (Wu Kiang, *Jen-min Jih-pao*, September 17, 1977). Saying that the theory is "complete" means no longer permitting anything but *commentaries* on it, and thus means putting forward a metaphysical proposition which forbids any elaboration or further research. It means trying to sterilize theory and cause it to wither, for if theory fails to advance it must retreat. In fact, what we see is an attempt to use Mao Tse-tung's theory against Mao Tse-tung. There is little difference between Wu Kiang's "complete theory" and Lin Piao's "absolute authority of Mao Tse-tung Thought."

Thus, at all levels we observe a "leap backward." This cannot be denied, unless one is unwilling to face reality because one feels, without being ready to admit it, that this reality compels us to examine problems we thought had been "solved," or would prefer not to believe exist (and I think that this is your attitude, my dear Neil Burton). Or else one denies that there has been a "leap backward" because one has always thought, or now thinks, that the Cultural Revolution was "harmful." This is, I believe, the view of most of the present leaders, who glorify in a one-sided way the achievements of the first seventeen years of the People's Republic of China (1949-66), while saying practically nothing about the *revolutionary phase* which opened in 1966. True, they do not venture to *repudiate expressly and openly* these last ten years of the Chinese Revolution, but their very silence on the revolutionary implications of those years confirms that they take up the position of the bourgeoisie.

The present situation being as I have described, it now remains to understand *how matters have got to this state.* This question is vital, for the answers involve lessons for the present and the future.

Actually, this question has several aspects. The first is essentially concerned with the course taken by events. It relates to the political conditions most immediately surrounding the defeat of the "revolutionary line," a defeat which became obvious after the death of Mao Tse-tung. Knowledge of these events, which in any case can at present be only fragmentary, informs us only partially as to the underlying causes of the defeat. It is nonetheless necessary for understanding the characteristic features of the present situation.

Remarks on the Meaning of the Expression
"Revolutionary Line"

Before proceeding to examine the conditions attending the defeat of the "revolutionary line," I think something needs to be said on the meaning of the expression I have put between quotation marks. This is necessary because the expression can be misleading, all the more so when the line is "personalized" by being called "Mao Tse-tung's political line."

In reality, an actual political line never "materializes" the orientations laid down by the highest levels of a party, even a centralized party, or by the leader who stands at the head of this party. The *actual* political line always depends on the social forces (classes, or social strata, or elements drawn from these classes and strata) which *give it life*.

It corresponds only partly to the orientations of principle to which it appeals, for it is heavily marked by the special aspirations and interests of these social forces. Their aspirations depend, *inter alia*, on the conception they have of the "interests of the community" — a conception which is inevitably affected by the *position* they occupy in the system of social relations. This implies that there can be a more or less considerable gap between the political line of principle proclaimed by the leading bodies of a party and the actual political line.[23] The latter depends fundamentally on the social forces which give it its real content, and whose interests, aspirations, and conceptions it materializes.

It is therefore wrong to identify a party's actual political line with the orientations of a particular leader or leading body. This line is not the form assumed by their "directives." It is the result of an ideological and political *intervention* in an *objective process*. It may modify the course taken by this process, but only within *limits* imposed by the relations of strength between classes, relations on which it exercises an influence which is far from being "sovereign."

The identification, in political practice, of an actual line with the guidance given by a leading political body or individual leader (even when this line *diverges* more or less profoundly from the guidance in question) is not necessarily due to "stratagems" or systematic "deception." It arises from the conditions under which political struggles take place when the only policy officially "legitimized" is that which is laid down by a supreme authority.

Thus the Chinese Communist Party accepts that the political line applied in China since the founding of the People's Republic is the line "defined by the party and by Chairman Mao," that is, the "basic line" of the party. This line is therefore considered to have been "applied" in the periods when Liu Shao-chi and Lin Piao wielded substantial power. Even in these periods, it is said, the "basic line" was being applied "in the main," despite "interferences" by an "enemy line," or "sabotage" of the official line.

Consequently, the *divergences* between the official orientations and the actual line are both admitted and denied. The resulting confusions are due to the very procedure (which is in fact an idealist method) whereby the actual political line is related, first and foremost, to a "system of ideas" and decisions taken "in the name of" these ideas, instead of being related explicitly to the social forces which embody the actual political line. It is true that, in dealing with current history, this procedure is often unavoidable, because *exposure* of the *social forces* which embody a given political line is not always possible.

These observations do not apply only to the political history of the People's Republic of China. They apply to all social formations in which the actual political line is *regarded as being defined and fixed by the highest instances of a ruling party*, and in which it appears as having been so fixed. This appearance, connected with the existence of certain political relations, may engender a *myth* of "united leadership" and "monolithism," or, as its counterpart, a myth of "totalitarianism."

The Soviet Communist Party has also constantly encountered the problem, *at once false and real*, of "divergences" between the proclaimed political line and the *actual* political line, these usually being spoken of as examples of "violation" of the line. In some periods this "violation" was attributed to "shortcomings in organizational work," as, for example, at the Seventeenth Congress of the CPSU in 1934, when it was said that "organization decides everything" (see the Russian report of this congress, published in Moscow in 1934, especially pp. 33 and 619). Later this "violation" was blamed on the activity of "enemies," on "sabotage," on "survivals from the past," and so forth. In any case, what matters is that there is both explicit admission of the conflict between the line of principle and the actual line (this being described as "violation") and an inability to "think" this conflict in terms of real social forces.

If we turn back to the political line which actually prevailed during the Cultural Revolution, we therefore would need to stress that this line—which, as a whole, was not repudiated by Mao, even though he may have criticized several aspects of it— was not simply the "materialization" of political orientations given in the resolutions of the Chinese Communist Party and the writings of its chairman. *In order to understand the real and complex social nature of this line,* one would need to undertake a *differentiated* analysis, and this is not at present feasible. Only such an analysis would show what the social forces (*classes* and *sections of classes*) were which actually "intervened," socially or ideologically, in the political scene. These social forces were the *"agents" of what appeared as the political line of Mao Tse-tung,* and which to a large extent determined the *content* of this line.

It is therefore only *with many reservations* that we can use the expression "Mao Tse-tung's political line" to describe the line which was dominant between 1966 and 1976.

We must not lose sight of the fact that using the name of a particular leader to describe a certain political line involves a number of negative consequences. Indeed, when the leader in question is held in high esteem, such use of his name can have a very intimidating effect. It tends to discourage critical analysis of the political line, to create a situation in which "argument from authority" takes the place of a thorough examination of the facts and principles. This substitution may entail profoundly harmful consequences. It contributes to engendering an atmosphere in which what certain leaders say is regarded as being "necessarily correct," and discourages the masses and the party members from putting forward their own opinions.

The use of the term "revolutionary line" also calls for reservations. Actually, any and every political line is marked by the social and political forces (which are not all revolutionary in character) that participate, directly or indirectly, in its application, and even in its elaboration. Despite these reserva tions, I use these expressions here because, *in the given conditions*, the principal aspect of the line which prevailed between 1966 and 1976 was such that we can say that this line was the most revolutionary and also the closest (in spite of enormous divergences) to *Mao Tse-tung's conceptions of principle*, which was why, in the main, *he gave it his support*.

Having said this, let us return to considering the conditions in which this line suffered defeat.

The Immediate Political Conditions of the Defeat of "Mao Tse-tung's Political Line" Following His Death

I shall say only a few words about these conditions. First, Hua Kuo-feng's accession to power resulted from a *coup d'état*. This *coup d'état* began a political turn leading to the substitution of a revisionist and bourgeois line for the previous revolutionary and proletarian line. The order of the most important events is well known. There were other events on which our information is scanty or inadequate. I shall confine myself to the following points.

Immediately after Mao's death on September 9, 1976, the unity of the leadership of the Chinese Communist Party around the political line followed until that time *did not seem* to be openly broken. All the leaders took part in the ceremonies in memory of Chairman Mao held between September 11 and 18, and Wang Hung-wen was a member of the Funeral Committee (*Peking Review*, no. 38, 1976).

On September 18, Hua Kuo-feng made a speech reaffirming the fundamental themes of the revolutionary line. He noted that classes and class contradictions persist throughout the transition to socialism. He reaffirmed the thesis of the special features of the class struggle during the transition. He quoted Mao's formulation concerning Teng Hsiao-ping and his supporters; "You are making the socialist revolution, and yet do not know where the bourgeoisie is. It is right in the Communist Party—those in power taking the capitalist road. The capitalist-roaders are still on the capitalist road" (*Peking Review*, no. 39, 1976).

In this same speech Hua Kuo-feng stated that the Cultural Revolution had "smashed the schemes of Liu Shao-chi, Lin Piao, and Teng Hsiao-ping for restoration, and criticized their counter-revolutionary revisionist line" (ibid.). He added that it was necessary to "deepen the struggle to criticize Teng Hsiao-ping and repulse the Right deviationist attempt to reverse correct verdicts" (ibid.).

The days that followed saw the appearance of signs of tension among the leaders. It seems that on September 19, Hua took possession of Mao Tse-tung's personal papers and on September 29 there was a stormy session (of the Political Bureau?) at which Hua accused the Four of having altered some of Mao's statements. However, on the evening of September 30 the entire leadership was present at a "forum" held in the hall on top of Tien An-men Gate.[24]

During the very first days of October one could observe, if one read the press attentively, the appearance of divergent formulations. Then on October 6 Hua Kuo-feng, relying on the security forces and on the military leaders of North China, carried out his *coup d'état*, arresting the Four (it is said that they are still alive). During these operations Mao Yuan-hsin, a nephew of Mao Tse-tung's, was killed, as was Ma Hsiao-liu, head of the Peking workers' militia.[25] On October 8, in the most dubious of circumstances, some members of established leading bodies having been deprived of their liberty and others having been threatened with arrest, Hua Kuo-feng had himself "appointed" chairman of the Central Committee and chairman of the Central Committee's Military Affairs Commission, while retaining the post of prime minister. At the same time, he had himself assigned the monopoly on publishing and interpreting the works of Mao Tse-tung. All these decisions were announced in the name of the "Central Committee," which in fact had not met.[26] From October 10 on, a campaign was launched against the Four, who were accused of "revisionism" and of "weaving plots and intrigues." At the same time, an appeal for discipline was issued.

For the moment, Hua's "appointment" to the chairmanship was reported discreetly in the newspapers.[27] Only on October 21 were great demonstrations announced, to "acclaim" the "appointment" of Hua and to "celebrate the crushing of the Gang of Four." Thereupon, in complete conflict with historical truth, it was declared that Mao had been against the Four. On October 28 Chang, Yao, and Wang were stripped of all their functions in Shanghai; criticism of Teng Hsiao-ping, however, remained officially on the agenda.[28]

The joint editorial in *Jen-min Jih-pao* and *Chiehfangchun Pao* on October 25 strove to "show" that the "Central Committee decision" appointing Hua Kuo-feng chairman of the party had been taken in conformity with a decision made on April 30, 1976, by Chairman Mao. This allegation testifies to the existence in the Chinese party of some doubts regarding the regularity of this appointment, so that it was necessary to endow Hua with a different form of "legitimacy," namely, designation by Chairman Mao himself. Actually, such "legitimacy" could not apply in a Communist Party that was operating in accordance with its own rules. Besides, there was nothing to base it on, for the phrase of Mao's that was now constantly quoted—"With you in charge, I'm at ease"—*does not indicate to whom it was addressed, nor what this person was "in charge" of.*

In any case, from the end of October on, Hua put himself forward as Mao's sole legitimate successor, and set in motion a sort of "cult" of his personality. Thereafter his photograph appeared increasingly frequently, side by side with Mao's and in the same format.[29]

Starting in November, calls for discipline became more frequent, and a decision was announced to reestablish "rational rules and regulations in the factories." At the same time a campaign of calumny was launched against the Four—a campaign so clearly mendacious that there is no need for any reply; it merely discredits those who are responsible for it.[30]

Criticism of Teng Hsiao-ping stopped at the end of November.[31] In December productivist slogans became increasingly more frequent.

In January 1977 various demonstrations calling for Teng's return were reported. In February the minister of foreign affairs, Huang Hua, said that Teng would return "at the opportune moment." In March Hua Kuo-feng proposed, at a working meeting of the Central Committee, that Teng again be given responsibilities. It was then that the campaigns of "socialist emulation" began, with the announcement of accelerated mechanization of agriculture. At that moment Teng seems to have returned to political activity *in practice*.

At the end of June 1977 *Jen-min Jih-pao* praised Teng's ideas, which had previously been criticized, and endorsed his criticisms of the revolutionary line (henceforth presented as the line of the Four).

The situation at the top had evolved in such a way that Teng now returned openly to political activity. At the third session of the Central Committee (July 16-21, 1977) Hua was officially appointed chairman and Teng recovered all his previous powers. At the Eleventh Party Congress (August 2-18, 1977) Teng made the closing speech.

Thus, sixteen months after having been removed from all his duties, Teng got them all back. The Chinese people did not receive any real explanation of what had happened. They were simply told that two mutually contradictory decisions had been adopted unanimously by the party's central bodies. The first decision was announced like this: the Political Bureau of the Central Committee of the Chinese Communist Party "unanimously agrees to dismiss Teng Hsiao-ping from all posts both inside and outside the party" (*Peking Review*, no. 15, 1976). The second was formulated as follows: the third plenary session of the Central Committee of the Chinese Communist Party "unanimously adopted the 'Resolution on Restoring Comrade Teng Hsiao-ping to his posts' " (*Peking Review*, no. 31, 1977).

But this about-face did not take place "peacefully." It was the culmination of an acute class struggle in which the security organs played a big part. Although official information regarding their role and the various forms of repression used is scarce, when we put together such information as we have, including information provided by foreigners who were in China until recently, it becomes apparent that repression was (and still is), being carried out on a large scale. In all the provinces for which we possess information there have been not only arrests but also executions, and the latter seem to have been exceptionally numerous.[32] The press, too, has emphasized the role played by the security organs, especially toward the end of 1977 (e.g., in *Jen-min Jih-pao*, November 27 and 28).

Throughout 1977 repression was accompanied by a mass "purge" of the party. Information is scarce here too, so that we cannot gauge the magnitude of the operation, but according to some travelers who have come back from China and who were able to talk with officials of a certain rank, it would appear that one-third of the cadres were "purged." These were mainly those cadres who had come up from the ranks during the Cultural Revolution. This purge is being accompanied by a mass return of those cadres who had been purged previously. Consequently, the Chinese Communist Party at the end of 1977 was much closer in the composition of its cadres to what it was in 1965 than to what it was in October 1976.

Parallel with the return of the Rightists we note that Teng Hsiao-ping's position is being strengthened: his close collaborators are taking over more and more key posts, notably in the Central Committee's department of organization (which decides appointments, transfers, promotions, and dismissals in all the party's bodies),[33] in other central departments, and in a number of provinces.

At the same time, stress is increasingly being laid on production, which "takes precedence over the class struggle" (*Jen-min Jih-pao*, December 12, 1977). This process is also accompanied by the creation of new targets for criticism. These targets have not yet been clearly designated, but it is possible to discern them amidst various changes of formulation. Thus the formulation calling for criticism of "Liu Shao-chi, Lin Piao, and the Gang of Four" is now often replaced by one which omits the name of Liu Shao-chi. It is now from time to time noted that "we need to counterattack not only against the Right but also against the 'Left' " — the last word being put between quotation marks to show that what is meant is not really Left. This

declaration seems aimed at opening the way for a new campaign of criticism, as *Jen-min Jih-pao* of December 12, 1977,
which carried it, added: "Not a few persons have proved incapable of distinguishing the real Left from the fake Left." At
the beginning of 1978 this campaign continues, especially in
the army paper, which attacks (without naming anyone) "those
who change direction with the wind," are experts in the
"180-degree turn,"[34] and try to escape from their own responsibilities by joining in the criticism of the Four. Should this
orientation be confirmed, it seems certain to lead to fresh
purges which would strike at those who were active in criticizing Teng and then showed the same zeal against the Four.[35]

This review of the "events" which accompanied and followed
the *coup d'état* of October 1976 is necessary if we are to
appreciate the immediate conditions under which the *coup
d'état* took place, and to obtain a partial view of some of its
consequences. But it does not explain *why* these "events"
took place—how they were determined by changes in
relations of strength between the classes and why these changes
occurred. The last section will attempt to answer some of these
questions.

*The Changes in the Relations of Strength Between the Classes
and the Victory of a Revisionist Line*

I have already disposed of the simplistic "explanation" according to which the new line of the Chinese Communist Party
was dictated by the "economic failure" of the line previously
followed. This explanation is fundamentally incorrect. In
reality, as we have seen, the overall economic balance sheet of
the years 1966-76 was a very positive one. One may, of course,
consider that it could, and even should, have been better, and
that in the years ahead there will have to be a certain speeding
up of the tempo of economic development, but there is absolutely nothing to prove that this speed-up could not have
been brought about without abandoning the revolutionary
line, provided that this line was rectified. That is why, as I see
it, this abandonment cannot be accounted for by "economic
necessities," but only by a reversal of relations of strength be-

tween the classes. In the absence of a real balance sheet of the years 1966-76 it is impossible (and pointless) to try and list the ways in which the previous line could or should have been rectified. Only a broad discussion and social experimentation (neither of which took place) would have made it possible concretely to eliminate the mistakes that were committed by deepening the revolutionary line.

One thing, in any case, is striking: in the municipality of Shanghai, where the revolutionary line was applied most coherently—with the least amount of interference from elements hostile to it, those who sabotaged it in practice while rallying to it in words—the "economic results" appear to have been excellent. Persons who have lived in China and worked in factories in Shanghai and in other cities generally report that in the Shanghai factories the atmosphere, as regards work and production, was generally as good as, and even, more often than not, better, than elsewhere.

However, the defeat of the revolutionary line did not come from nowhere. Nor can it be explained merely by referring to the "skill," "cunning," or "unscrupulousness" of the opponents of this line. These factors certainly played a part, but they were not the essential ones. If the line suffered defeat, this was because, in a certain way, *it had failed*. It is quite vital to consider *the nature and causes of this failure*, which, ultimately, are to be sought on the plane of relations between the classes. Examination of this question ought to furnish answers with very wide application, affecting not China alone.

I repeat: for the moment we can give only partial and provisional answers, but these will perhaps serve as the starting point for a wider ranging study, which will include criticism of what may prove to be mistaken in the answers being offered here.

It must first be said that the principal obstacle to our presenting adequately developed answers *is the absence of a class analysis of present-day China*. This is a serious and significant fact: *the Chinese Communist Party has not produced such an analysis*. Some of the Four tried to fill this *vacuum*, but they did not succeed. They were prevented from doing so by an inadequate grasp of the theoretical concepts needed for a class analysis of a social formation in transition. This inadequacy was shown in the tendency to define the Chinese bourgeoisie of today not by reference to its place in production relations, but by its ideology or its political line—or, at best, by distribution relations conceived as an effect of bourgeois right. At bottom, the bourgeoisie was seen as a product of the superstructure and not of the economic base.

This inadequacy had its source in the employment of the concept (which contradicts Marxism) of "socialist ownership," itself conceived as an effect wrought upon the economic base by a change in the superstructure.

This theoretical inadequacy had many causes, in particular the absence of a broad discussion free from ready-made formulas, and the barrage directed by the opponents of the revolutionary line against any attempt to develop such a class analysis. The bourgeoisie defended itself. It is no accident that one of the "charges" now brought against the Four is that they wanted to carry out a class analysis of China—this being pointless, it is said, since such an analysis had long since been made by Mao Tse-tung.

While the absence of a class analysis of present-day China constitutes an obstacle to a full understanding of the changes which have come about in class relations during recent years, it is also—and this is a much more serious matter—*one of the reasons for the failure of the revolutionary line.* One cannot transform class relations in a revolutionary way if one does not know what these relations are. Lacking this knowledge, a ruling party can only, in the end, maintain the status quo while endeavoring to "modernize the economy."[36]

One cannot emphasize too strongly the gravity of a situation in which there is no party document presenting a materialistic analysis of the classes and social strata in China today, the social differentiation within the working class,[37] and within the people's communes.[38] The absence of a concrete analysis of the new class relations is reflected in the resort to stereotyped labeling. Examples of this are numerous. Thus, more than twenty years after the founding of the people's communes, the categories (which had meaning at the time when the communes were founded) of poor peasants, middle peasants, upper-stratum middle peasants, rich peasants, and landlords are still being used.[39] But today these categories no longer serve as anything but a ridiculous substitute for an analysis of the *present* classes and social strata. Similarly, instead of a real analysis of the class bases of the different lines, the lines being "criticized" are always denounced in terms of *the same stock labels*. The result is mere repetition of *the same accusations addressed to upholders of opposing lines*.

Here is a typical example. In 1976 an article entitled "A Great Victory" (*Jen-min Jih-pao*, April 10) declared that Teng Hsiao-ping's social base was made up of "the capitalist-roaders in the party" who were "connected with the bourgeoisie and the unreformed landlords, rich peasants, counter-revolutionaries, bad elements, and Rightists in society" (*Peking Review*, no. 16, 1976). As another example, in 1977 Hua Kuo-feng, who had accepted this "analysis," declared in his report to the Eleventh Congress, with Teng Hsiao-ping by his side, that the Four were "typical representatives within our party of landlords, rich peasants, counter-revolutionaries, and bad elements, as well as of the old and new bourgeois elements. . . ." (*Peking Review*, no. 35, 1977).

Such formulations reveal the leadership's inability or refusal to put before the party and the people a *serious* class analysis of the political lines being criticized. If it be supposed that such an analysis has indeed been made but has been kept "secret" (which is unlikely), this would be unworthy of a party which claims to be guiding the masses. Actually, there is every reason to assume that the leadership of the Chinese Communist Party has not carried out any fundamental analysis, and consequently has been unable to do more than repeat the same clichés.[40]

Of course, the fact that the struggles over vital questions which have divided the party in recent years have not been guided by a serious and rigorous class analysis does not mean that these struggles have not corresponded to *profound class cleavages*. But it does imply that these cleavages have been apprehended *intuitively* and *globally*, and so without subtlety. Under these conditions it is impossible to *trace correct lines of demarcation*, to deal properly with the *secondary contradic-*

tions (which may thus assume an antagonistic character), and, therefore, to arrange *compromises* corresponding to the *class alliances* demanded if the transition to socialism is to be carried through.

To a large extent, the history of the Cultural Revolution is that of an immense forward thrust (effected between May 1966 and February 1967),[41] followed by a series of retreats and fresh advances. The retreats were mainly due to the Left's inability to conclude the essential compromises and forge the necessary class alliances. The first retreats of the Cultural Revolution were blamed by Mao Tse-tung upon this inability, which affected not only relations between political forces but also relations between the classes themselves.[42]

A few phrases of Mao Tse-tung's which, isolated from their context and surrounded by appropriate commentaries, are now presented as *criticisms* of the Four are actually pieces of *advice* given to them—not to isolate themselves, to avoid sectarianism, not to act hastily. Such advice is radically different from the criticism addressed by Mao Tse-tung to the supporters of the revisionist line, such as Liu Shao-chi or Teng Hsiao-ping.

Apart from tactical problems (which concern relations between political forces), one of the factors which, it seems to me, played a decisive role in the defeat of the revolutionary line was its inability to deal correctly with the problem of the intellectuals and so, also, of the cadres. One of the results of this inability was that the Four often appeared more apt to *impose* their views and get rid of their opponents than to implement a fully constructive political line. The supporters of the revolutionary line showed themselves able to build various *forms of alliance* between the working masses and the intellectuals (in particular, in the different forms of "three-in-one combination"), but they did not always manage to *deal correctly with the contradictions within this alliance*. Consequently, they tended to *substitute coercion for political leadership*.

Antagonisms therefore developed, which engendered, on the part of some of the supporters of the Left, measures of harassment and bullying and even acts of repression which were often directed not against real enemies but against persons who were merely suspected of being enemies. These practices were frequently the work of elements that were not truly revolutionary—opportunists who had outwardly rallied to the Left and were seeking mainly to exploit the Left's prestige for their own ends.

Furthermore, even the leaders of the Left took a sectarian attitude toward scientists and artists. Consequently, obstacles were placed in the way of the development of scientific and technical knowledge and of the full progress of literary and artistic activity. The right to read foreign periodicals and books was narrowly restricted (which also reflected the contamination of some of the activists who had rallied to the revolutionary line by a populist and even xenophobic ideology). On the pretext of exercising strict supervision of publications and of all literary, cinematic, theatrical, and similar activities, the number of new works allowed to appear was kept small. In the scientific domain the number of works published was drastically reduced and most scientific journals ceased to appear. Even access to libraries was severely restricted.

As I have said, it may be that some of these measures were taken by opponents of the revolutionary line who, while claiming to act in its name, were in fact trying to do it harm. In any case, measures of this kind not only inflicted pointless damage on the development of science and technology, as well as of cultural activity, but were felt by the intellectuals as bullying and were probably in the end condemned by a section of the masses. Under such conditions it became inevitable that a majority of the intellectuals declined to support the revolutionary line, or only gave it lip service.

The supporters of the revolutionary line did not correct in good time practices that led to the development of contradictions with the intellectuals, and were thus drawn into the infliction of one measure of coercion and repression after another. These measures have been described too often for it to be necessary for me to recapitulate them here. Even if such descriptions are exaggerated, there can be no doubt that, basically, they correspond to some reality.

To sum up the foregoing, I think we can accept the formulation of W. Aschmoneit when he writes, under the heading "Revolutionizing by Coercion," "The alliance between the intelligentsia and the working classes did not take shape sufficiently, and to some extent there was even a deepening of mutual distrust and lack of understanding."[43]

As soon as the element of coercion enters into what ought to be an alliance, it tends to spread. In the end, coercion was brought to bear upon a section of the masses as well, and gave rise to discontent—for example, among the young people who were compelled to go and live in country areas, often without being convinced that they should, or being adequately prepared for the move, and also among their families.[44]

Unity of the masses therefore failed to develop. With increasing frequency, instead of the masses being allowed to express themselves, "speakers" appeared, acting instead and independently of them. Each time this happened the results obtained were unsound and the ground was prepared for a revisionist counteroffensive conducted under the banner of "liberalization."

No one who has not lived in China in this period can draw up a real balance sheet of these years. It is possible, however, to identify some *characteristic features* of these struggles, and, on this basis, to understand why they ended in the defeat of the revolutionary line.

One of the characteristics of those struggles has certainly been the *sectarian* way in which they were usually conducted. This sectarianism was due in part to the lack of a real analysis of classes which would have made it possible to draw correct lines of demarcation and form alliances. It was partly, also, the result of a schematic conception of Marxism which culminated in *dogmatism*. To a large extent this reflected the continued influence of the *degenerated* forms of Bolshevik ideology which developed during the 1930s and which culminated in the *transformation of Marxism into its opposite.*[45]

Chinese revisionism also came under this influence, but it did not conflict with that tendency's own aims, in contrast to the case of the revolutionary line, which lacked the theoretical conceptions it needed in order to develop its activity in a fully coherent way. Revisionism in China was not in the least embarrassed by this situation: on the contrary, it was able, as a result, to make use of conceptions that were both *dogmatic* and *eclectic*.

This eclecticism made the revisionist line *seem less coercive*. Accordingly, when Mao Tse-tung died, the discontent of the intellectuals, together with a certain lassitude among the masses, led a section of the latter (who, moreover, feared that there might be civil war) to rally to the revisionist line — *after* the supporters of this line had effected their *coup d'état*.

One of the characteristics of the struggles of the last few years, which helps explain why the revolutionary line was defeated, has been the intensely personal aspect they have assumed. This personalization of the struggles culminated in a veritable "cult of Mao." This cult may have briefly played a certain positive role, but, all things considered, it was a profoundly negative phenomenon: it enabled clever revisionist leaders to hide behind the trust that Mao is supposed to have shown them, to speak "in his name," or to proclaim themselves his "continuators." The examples of Lin Piao and Hua Kuofeng show that this is not merely a hypoethetical possibility.

The possibility in question is due to the fact that when struggles are personalized, instead of manifesting themselves mainly as conflicts over *problems of principle* and *lines*, they assume the appearance (despite *general* declarations which present them as being struggles between different lines) of *personal combat between individuals who are out to get positions*, and this applies at every level.

Moreover, this appearance is obviously a factor in reality. The slogan "Seize political power!" has often led to political struggle becoming transformed into a hunt for positions,[46] a hunt in which personal attacks on those occupying these positions have often played a bigger part than the struggle over principles. However, the substitution of conflicts between persons for the struggle to transform class relations could only result, in the end, in producing indifference and weariness among the masses, since the latter could not see how their living and working conditions were affected by conflicts of this sort. The supporters of the revisionist line played upon this lassitude, putting themselves forward as those who would restore "order" and "tranquillity." Actually, as soon as they had taken power at the center, they threw themselves into the worst sort of persecutions, purges, and hunts for positions, but they did this with less publicity, acting behind the backs of the masses.

To all this something else can be added, namely, the often *hermetic* character of the political conflicts. I will give only one example. The "Pi-Lin Pi-Kung" campaign (criticizing Lin Piao and Confucius) appears to have been aimed at several targets, at different times and depending on who was taking part. Among the targets were not only Lin Piao and Confucius, but also Chou En-lai, the Four, Teng Hsiao-ping, and perhaps others as well. Only a few people, though, could make out the meaning of a "discussion" such as this: for the rest, its pursuit and the obligation to "take part" could only, in the end, become unbearable.

The *hermeticism* of certain struggles reflected the fact that those promoting them *were not really trying to get the masses to take part*. These struggles were waged between the leaders, who "appealed to the masses" in order to obtain their support; but the content of what was at stake was seldom clearly explained. The use of the same labels to denounce persons who advocated profoundly different political lines was, to some extent, an aspect of the hermeticism. Former leaders were held up as objects for the wrath of the masses by using all-purpose labels, that is, *without really explaining to the masses what was at stake*, and so without helping them to break into the political arena and hold their ground. In this connection, the episode of the Shanghai Commune is particularly significant.

The Shanghai Commune: The Theoretical and Practical Implications of Its Rapid Disappearance

Here we must go back in time. This is all the more necessary because the Shanghai Commune tends to be passed over, whereas it possesses considerable importance, both theoretical and practical. I shall first recall certain facts.

From November 1966 onward Shanghai (as well as some other industrial towns, notably Tientsin and places in the Northeast) saw a multiplication in the number of factory committees devoted to the Cultural Revolution. These committees established "dual power" in the enterprises. They were a development ratified by a twelve-point directive from the central group of the Cultural Revolution.[47]

In the factories of Shanghai, the power of the Cultural Revolution committees was thus established alongside that of the production groups, which were made up primarily of cadres. At the end of December the latter disintegrated, while the factory committees developed into mass revolutionary organizations (called "headquarters"). Although these had difficulty in agreeing among themselves, they all challenged the authority of the existing municipal council, which they accused of revisionism. In early January 1967, after meetings which over a million workers attended, the municipal council collapsed.[48]

On January 9, thirty-two organizations jointly issued what was called an "urgent notice" which set forth a series of rules and apparently prepared the way for a new form of governing authority. The whole of the Chinese press published this document, and it was held up as a model by Mao Tse-tung himself. *Jen-min Jih-pao* of January 22, commenting on it, noted: "Of all the ways for the revolutionary masses to take their destiny into their own hands, in the final analysis the only way is to take power! Those who have power have everything; those who are without power have nothing. . . . We, the worker, peasant, and soldier masses, are the indisputable masters of the new world!"[49] On the walls of the city appeared the slogan: "All power to the Commune!"

Nevertheless, developments took their time. It was not until February 5 that the commune was proclaimed, at a meeting attended by a million workers. The speakers declared that "the municipal party committee and the city council of Shanghai had been destroyed and that a new organ of power had been established, in keeping with the doctrines of Chairman Mao and the principles of the dictatorship of the proletariat. . . ."[50]

However, the Shanghai Commune was not hailed in the central press, any more than was the formation of communes in other cities, such as Taiyuan. Without being officially repudiated, the commune was not, so to speak, "recognized" by the central authority. Some twenty days afterwards, it ceased to exist, with the birth of the Shanghai Revolutionary Committee, presided over by Chang Chun-chiao, who had taken part in the work of the Shanghai Commune, in accordance with the suggestion of the central group and with the approval of all the founding organizations.

Thus, in Shanghai as in other cities, the commune form, though it had been mentioned in the sixteen-point declaration, was dropped and replaced by that of the revolutionary committee.

No real argument justifying this change has ever been set forth. A variety of reasons have been given, mainly in Chang Chun-chiao's speech of February 24, in which he alluded to Mao Tse-tung's remarks on the creation of the Shanghai Commune.[51] According to Chang, Mao Tse-tung did not question the principle of the commune, but he did question whether the correct procedure had been followed in forming it. He doubted, moreover, whether the model inspired by the Paris Commune could be adopted anywhere but in Shanghai, China's most advanced working-class center. He also wondered about the international problems that would result from the proclamation of communes all over China. These observations were not very convincing, and took the form of questions rather than arguments. In any case, they did not lead to a condemnation of the commune, but were only an appeal for caution and prudence.

Actually, the principal problem raised by Mao was that of the party. He seems to have been very disturbed by the role assigned to the cadres, and by the tendency of some of the rebels to "overthrow all those in responsible positions." He asked the question: "Do we still need the party?" And he answered: "I think that we need it because we need a hard core, a bronze matrix, to strengthen us on the road we still have to travel. You can call it what you like, Communist Party or Socialist Party, but we must have a party. This must not be forgotten."

The question arises as to how the revolutionary leaders of the Chinese Communist Party, who had supported the political form of the commune, went back, in practice, to their previous attitude, claiming that China was not "ready" for this political form. How did they thereby open up a new course, which was to be marked by a series of retreats interrupted by partial, but increasingly less effective, counteroffensives?

In terms of the concrete unfolding of the Cultural Revolution, two sets of facts need to be taken into consideration. First, the various revolutionary organizations (in Shanghai and elsewhere) were apparently incapable of uniting. They tended to clash, often and violently, and to engage in efforts to outdo each other, efforts which risked causing confusion and mass elimination of honest and devoted cadres. Mao Tse-tung described this situation in July 1967, when he remarked on the inability shown by the most militant supporters of the Cultural Revolution to unite and to ally with all those with whom they ought to come to an agreement.[52]

The second set of facts is the negative reaction of the majority of party members at the highest level to the situation that developed at the beginning of 1967. These party members did not, in the main, take up revolutionary positions. Without saying so openly, they were hostile to the Cultural Revolution. And because they were a majority,[53] their calls for "moderation" were listened to: had this not happened, it would have been all over with the unity and even with the very existence of the party.

The attitude of many veterans of the revolution was epressed in Tan Chen-lin's speech at an enlarged session of the Political Bureau in January 1967, when he said: "Do you still need the leadership of the party? Do you want to destroy all the old cadres? I speak here in the name of all the veterans of the revolution, and I would rather be jailed or beheaded than be a silent witness to the humiliation of so many of our old comrades."[54]

This attitude on the part of most of the old cadres, and the desire to maintain the unity and existence of the party, led the Political Bureau to "narrow the front of attack" and "designate individual targets": Liu Shao-chi, Teng Hsiao-ping, and a few other officials. Another result was that an exceptional role was given to the People's Liberation Army and its then leader, Lin Piao. Thereafter it was the PLA, operating through its "propaganda teams for Mao Tse-tung Thought," that was to "recognize" the genuinely Left rank-and-file committees, guide them toward unifying action, and with them dominate the whole movement.[55]

These decisions led to the withering away of the mass movement and to an increase in the influence of the PLA leaders in the apparatus of the party and of the state.[56] In 1969, at the Ninth Party Congress, the PLA leaders played a decisive role. Of the twenty-five members elected to the Political Bureau, fourteen were PLA generals. The *mass movements* characteristic of the first years of the Cultural Revolution were replaced by *criticism campaigns organized from above*. In 1971 the danger that the PLA leaders, grouped around Lin Piao, presented to the revolutionary trend was so great that Lin Paio was brusquely eliminated. But this did not make the revolutionary trend the majority trend in the party: its representatives constituted only about one-third of the members of the Political Bureau.

The supporters of the revolutionary line did not manage to strengthen their position in the party sufficiently to prevent comebacks by increasing numbers of Rightist and revisionist elements. Finally, the *coup d'état* of October 1976, in which the PLA and the security services played a decisive part, was the culmination, in the forefront of the political stage, of a process which had been going on for years. This process was favored by the priority given to forms of organization led from above over mass movements with many different forms of organization. It was connected to the abandonment of the political form of the commune.

The unfolding of events is not enough, however, to explain either this abandonment or the eventual defeat of the revolutionary line. Explanation of these facts calls for study of the problem of the party's relations with the mass organizations, and especially with organizations of the commune type, consttuting *organs of the power of the working masses.* There was much that was contradictory in these relations. For one thing, the working masses were far from being spontaneously united and active. This circumstance was expressed in the development of contradictions among the masses, and it made it necessary to wage an ideological struggle to enable the proletarian and advanced elements of the masses to play an effective leading role. Here there arises the problem of the role to be played by a revolutionary party amid the contradictions that may split the masses and even bring about conflict between the different ideological and political trends which appear among them.

The party's contradictory relations with the masses also bring up this question: Is power in the hands of the masses, of their organizations and advanced elements, or is it in the party's hands? Or, putting it another way, is power wielded *by* the working people or is it wielded *for* them (assuming that the ruling party can remain in the service of the working people without being placed under effective control by them)?

For Marx, in *The Civil War in France*, the commune is the organ of power, the political form of the dictatorship of the proletariat. Similarly, for Lenin, in *State and Revolution*, the soviets are the organs of power of the working people. In these two works the leading role of a revolutionary party is not even mentioned. In 1919 Lenin noted, as a negative fact, that the soviets were not, as they should have been, "organs of government by the working people" but "organs of government *for* the working people by the advanced section of the proletariat, but not by the working people as a whole."[57] This situation was not destined to change, and led to the complete loss of power by the Soviet working people.

In the sixteen-point decision of August 8, 1966, the Chinese Communist Party raised the same problem, though in less clearcut fashion. On the one hand, reference was made to the system of the Paris Commune, and it was said that the new forms of organization of the masses emerging from the Cultural Revolution "are organs of power of the Proletarian Cultural Revolution" (point 9). On the other hand, it was said that, thanks to these forms of organization, "under the leadership of the Communist Party the masses are educating themselves." These two formulations are not contradictory provided that power is really in the hands of the masses, that the party's leadership is exercised through the work of its members, and that this work takes the form of persuasion and explanation and not of the wielding of an authority imposed by coercive means. As was said in the communiqué of the Central Committee of the Chinese Communist Party adopted on August 12, 1966, "the key to the success of this great Cultural Revolution is to have faith in the masses, rely on them, boldly arouse them, and respect their initiative. . . . Be pupils of the masses before becoming their teachers. Don't be afraid of disorder. . . . Oppose the creation of a lot of restrictions to tie the hands of the masses."

The substitution of revolutionary committees for the commune form in Shanghai, the role accorded to the PLA in choosing representatives of the masses, and the way in which these representatives were appointed to the revolutionary committees, all implied abandonment of the orientation which had been explicitly adopted in August 1966.

This abandonment corresponded, as we have seen, to an evolution unfavorable to the revolutionary line in the relation of forces within the party leadership.[58] It was also due to the inability of the mass organizations to unite and to avoid sectarian practices, both in dealings with each other and in their treatment of numerous cadres. This evolution and these practices seem to have been connected with the predominance of a certain conception of the role of the party, one that aimed at imposing its views on the masses rather than at convincing them. They were connected, too, with the "personalizing" of the struggles. These two phenomena cannot be separated from the weakness of the analyses made of the nature of the dominant social relations during the transition to socialism, for these relations were declared to be "socialist."[59]

That assertion hinders the development of long-term struggles to *transform social relations* (since these are seen as being "already socialist"). It tends also to substitute personal conflict for such struggles, and the development of these conflicts brings petty-bourgeois elements to the forefront and tends to thrust into the background militants from the working class who are not interested in a "hunt for positions." Under these conditions the supporters of the revolutionary line were sometimes led to try and find support among petty-bourgeois elements (which were inevitably unstable) and sometimes, so as to avoid the chaos that could result from the intervention of these petty-bourgeois elements, to turn toward the cadres of the PLA, or toward the civilian cadres, which ended by favoring the revisionist elements and weakening the revolutionary line.

These are, I think, some of the factors which explain the *limits* that the Cultural Revolution came up against, and some of the reasons for the *defeat* the revolutionary line suffered after the death of Mao Tse-tung.

The "Ideological Heritage" and Its Active Role

The preceding remarks relate, in part, to the "ideological heritage" derived from the degenerated form of the Bolshevik ideological formation dating from the end of the 1930s. They relate also, as regards the "personalizing" of struggles, to the survival of elements of feudal ideology, to which China remains heir today.

It is necessary to ask *why these "heritages" have survived.* What are the elements in social relations and the dominant social practices which enable these "heritages" to remain active? Why has criticism of these degenerate forms of the Bolshevik ideology (though it was begun to a considerable extent in some of Mao Tse-tung's writings) not been fully developed, and why has it not *brought about the dominance of practices which this criticism calls for?*

It is obviously not easy to answer such wide-ranging questions. Here I can only offer a few reflections, or, more precisely, some fragmentary results of my thinking about the problem of how they should be answered.

To begin with, I note that certain social relations, the reproduction of which restricted the functioning of Mao Tse-tung's line and facilitated the revisionist counteroffensive, were not subjected to systematic criticism and practical attack. At the heart of these relations lie (1) the *hierarchical relations* (more precisely, the bourgeois political relations) existing in the machinery of party and state, (2) the *departmentalizing* of the different parts of the state machine, and (3) the *separation* between the party's basic organizations, which cannot normally communicate with each other and are linked only with the organs above them. This separation and departmentalizing endows the higher organs of the party with substantial power and ensures the reproduction of relations typical of bourgeois apparatuses, relations marked by the existence of *hierarchy* and *secrecy*. It renders the masses incapable of *appointing* and *recalling* officials. Consequently, the latter cannot be servants of the people, for they belong to a network of apparatuses which dominate the masses.

There is an economic basis to these political relations, namely, the capitalist production relations which have not been transformed, but which react in turn upon the conditions of economic and social reproduction. They make it possible for *control of the means of production* to be concentrated in a few hands. In this connection, the carrying through of the partial changes in the *immediate production process* imposed by the Cultural Revolution was blocked by the *absence of a fundamental transformation of the process of reproduction*. In its essentials (the fixing of rates of accumulation, the allocation of investments between sectors, etc.) this continued to take place outside of the control by the immediate producers, who were at best "consulted" on this or that detailed aspect of the economic plans. The *separation* of the immediate producers from their means of production was thus only overcome to a slight degree, and therefore capitalist and commodity relations continued to be reproduced.

The economic counterpart of the *bourgeois* political relations was constituted, also, by an *inequality in distribution relations*. This was not merely a matter of an eight-grade wage system but of some thirty grades in the hierarchy of payments. It also involved the *privileges* enjoyed by the cadres of the party and the state, which increased as one rose in the hierarchy.

These privileges involved, for example, the use of a service automobile, more spacious and comfortable housing, and even, above a certain level, a villa and access to special shops (for clothes and certain consumer durables such as refrigerators, radios, TV sets, cameras, tape recorders, etc.). At the level of the central leadership, these privileges could extend to possession of several villas, free use of an airplane for personal trips, and so on.[60]

The privileges of the cadres have been particularly denounced over the last eighteen months, in a campaign of "big-character posters" which has not been directed exclusively against the Four, as the authorities might have wished. The most critical of these posters have been quickly torn down.[61] They have nonetheless contributed to making known a reality which implies that the cadres of different levels enjoy "legal" privileges and live, at their respective levels of the hierarchy, *in a different world* from that of the masses.

Moreover, the existence of these "legal" privileges is a source of "illegal" privileges and advantages, of everything that can be acquired, especially by the middle-ranking cadres, "through the back door," as they say in China: the opportunity to have a villa built illegally, favors for the children of cadres (to enable them to go to university, to ensure that the local cadres in the villages where they are sent see that they are not assigned to work of too arduous a kind, etc.). It is impossible to estimate the magnitude of these "illegal" privileges (which are a consequence of the "legal" ones), but according to recent "big-character posters" they are relatively extensive, while being both combated and tolerated by the state apparatuses which are supposed to have it as their duty to prevent their appearance. Actually, the members of these very apparatuses enjoy these same privileges, and so they attack them only in a very limited way.

It must be added, finally, that the existence of bourgeois political relations and of *a high degree of centralization* favors *self-recruitment by the political leaders*, especially when, under "democratic centralism," the centralism heavily outweighs the democracy. This self-recruitment is expressed, for instance, in the *cooptation* of the members of the Central Committee and the Political Bureau. It easily leads to the formation of "cliques" and to nepotism.

It must be acknowledged that the predominance of centralism over democracy is linked (so far as forms of organization and political practice are concerned) with *prohibition of complete freedom of expression in the party*. It is to the point to recall that in the Bolshevik Party a ban like this was introduced only comparatively late, by means of a onesided and incorrect interpretation of a resolution of the Tenth (1921) Party Congress. In principle, *this resolution was not intended to prevent freedom for the expression of divergent points of view*,[62] and it was adopted, moreover, only as a *temporary measure*, which the circumstances of a particular moment could alone justify.[63]

The existence of bourgeois political relations, accompanied by a system of privileges, forms one of the *bases* on which degenerate and altered forms of the Bolshevik ideology are reproduced. (The forms of the Bolshevik ideology which resulted from the transformation of this ideology during the 1930s served in the Soviet Union to defend similar privileges.)[64] I think that the existence of these relations explains — *given the absence of a mass movement radically challenging them* — why the criticisms made in China of Stalin's "mistakes" *were never pursued consistently and given systematic form*.

At this point the questions raised earlier come up once more, but in another form: *why did no mass movement arise to challenge radically the system of bourgeois political relations and centralization*, although on several occasions criticism of this system was widely developed among the masses?

No single answer can be given to this question. The elements of an answer which I can offer are as follows, being put forward in a hypothetical and problematic form.

A first element of the explanation is to be found in the *objective function which the existing system fulfills, within certain limits*. This function consists, fundamentally, in ensuring *a certain form of unity in the reproduction of social relations*. This system cannot, therefore, really be *destroyed* without being replaced by *another form of unity.* One does not truly destroy anything unless one puts something in its place. But *this other form of unity can be discovered only by the social movement itself.* It cannot be "invented" by theory. *Social eperimentation* combined with *theoretical criticism* is here indispensable. The limitations imposed in this sphere upon mass social experimentation blocked the road to the discovery of forms of unity which could ensure a dominant role for the mass organizations, while not ruling out the possibility of a renovated and transformed party playing a leading ideological role.

Secondly, it must be noted that the fear felt by the masses themselves that the existing form of unity might collapse contributed to preventing any radical challenge to the prevailing political relations. Thus, the Shanghai Commune could neither be maintained nor presented as a model. It was abandoned without this arousing any mass protest. Finally, the revolutionary committees increasingly constituted, de facto, a *transformed form of existence of bourgeois political relations*, under the pressure of the bourgeois class struggle and through the reproduction of a number of *social practices*.

It is a question, in particular, of the *methods of leadership, which are in contradiction with the development of genuine mass democracy.* This latter requires that neither the *free expression of opinions* nor the *multiform organization* of the masses be hindered. However, diversity in the forms of intervention by the working people (through the multiplication of "rebel organizations" in the first phase of the Cultural Revolution, the use of "big-character posters" expressing a great variety of opinions, and the appearance of uncensored publications by rebel organizations) was only a passing phase. The party cadres who were not criticized, and even those who themselves emerged from the Cultural Revolution quickly set limits to these forms of intervention. They gradually replaced those who spoke for the different trends among the masses with "representatives" of the masses: these "representatives" were gradually *consolidated in their positions and integrated with the established apparatuses.* They were thus cut off from their base, and by subjecting this base to *repetitious practices*, they blocked the initiative of the working people and the expression of criticism.

Such methods of leadership run counter to the advance toward socialism, which calls for *thoroughgoing democracy*. These methods were consolidated by fear of seeing the unity of the reproduction process broken while the rise of new forms of unity still seemed uncertain. They were consolidated also by the absorption of the cadres who had emerged from the Cultural Revolution into a system of privileges which had not been fundamentally challenged—a system which some of these cadres sought to preserve in order to benefit from it.

The imposition of antidemocratic practices contradicts the pursuit of a really revolutionary line, as well as some of Mao Tse-tung's watchwords: "It is right to revolt against reactionaries"; "Going against the stream is a principle of Marxism-Leninism." Such practices justify the analyses made by Mao when in 1964 he said that the Chinese Communist Party was no more revolutionary "in its essence" than any other party, that a party which has been a revolutionary party can always change into its opposite and become counter-revolutionary and fascist,[65] from which follows the need for the party to maintain its leading role not through coercion but through ideological struggle, accepting the existence of other political parties.[66]

For all these reasons, the predominance of antidemocratic practices contradicts the requirements for the revolution's advance.

Ultimately, as we know, only the working people can accomplish their emancipation. Preventing progress in the activity of the masses means opposing the continuation of the revolution. The latter cannot go forward when the freedom of organization of the working people is hindered, when attempts are made to *impose* upon the masses, and upon the members of the party, "unified thinking," whether this be done by persecuting and repressing those who "think differently" from the leaders or by organizing discussion meetings which turn into a mere repetition of what is regarded, at a particular moment, as being "correct." Pursuit of the revolution also becomes impossible when obstacles are placed in the way of the activity of the masses by establishing a monopoly of information or by distorting historical truth (for such distortion prevents the masses from learning their own history, and therefore from acting on the present situation in a wellinformed way). Eventually, these various hindrances can only lead to defeats in the struggle for the emancipation of the masses, for the development of social experimentation and of scientific knowledge,[67] with a general mastery of this knowledge and political action based upon it.

A revolutionary line which does not respect these requirements, or does not succeed in ensuring that they are respected, is not completely self-consistent. Whatever temporary gains it may make, it is doomed to suffer defeat in the end. In China this defeat has taken the form of a *coup d'état* by the supporters of the present revisionist line, with its "liberal" demagogy and its deceitful economic promises.

The Present Course and the Prospects Before It

The present course is, indeed, marked not only by economism and productivism but also by "liberal" demagogy. While repression directed against the masses and against the revolutionaries is being practiced on a large scale, the talk is of "a hundred flowers," or even of "a thousand flowers." But these "flowers" are destined mainly for the intellectuals[68] — on condition that they agree, where essentials are concerned, to repeat whatever the party says. It is being said over and over again, in fact, that "obedience to the party leadership is necessary for the victory of the proletariat": the idea (which corresponds to reality) that the party could have got into the hands of a revisionist leadership is ruled out by what is assumed.

Oddly enough, the present leadership is restoring a semblance of life to the old mummified parties which no longer represent anything, since they no longer recruit.[69] This is an attempt to seem to take account of what Mao said about the need for mutual supervision by the parties; it is also, and mainly, a way of reassuring the former intellectual and bourgeois circles whom these parties are supposed to represent.

While the new leadership of the party is trying to conciliate the intellectuals and the former bourgeoisie, it is tightening up labor discipline in the factories and the people's communes, and restricting, in practice, access by worker and peasant children to higher education.

All this is being done in the name of "economic growth," with the workers being allowed to hope that they will soon reap the fruits of rapid increase in "modern" means of production and "sophisticated" weapons, which entails an enormous effort of accumulation, so that, apart from a few crumbs, the principal "fruits" that the working people will reap will be an intensification of labor and increased subjection to the orders of the cadres, technicians, and specialists — that is, the strengthening of the dictatorship of the state bourgeoisie.

The true class nature of the present leadership of the Chinese Communist Party is also revealed in its international policy. Here the consequences of the "Three Worlds" theory, as it has been worked out by Teng Hsiao-ping, are being carried further and further.[70] This has been shown, for example, in the backing given to French imperialist intervention in Africa and in support of the most reactionary regimes: those of Mobutu, Bokassa, and Idi Amin in Africa, that of Pinochet in Latin America.[71] The class significance of this support is all the greater because it is even contrary to the interests of China as a nation. It is felt by the people as a demonstration of contempt for their democratic and national aspirations, and it helps to strengthen the prestige of social-imperialism, which, on the whole, maneuvers more skillfully (even while intervening alongside Ethiopian colonialism, against the national liberation struggles of the Somalis of the Ogaden and the Eritrean people). To be convinced of the negative consequences for China of the foreign policy it is pursuing, one needs only to talk with *working people of the Third World*, in whose eyes China's prestige is now at its lowest.

It should also be noted that China's present international policy is continued in a *foreign trade* policy which tends to integrate China more closely in the world market,[72] so that the scale on which China's productive forces develop must depend more and more upon the fluctuations in this market. Thus, to the factors of crisis implicit in a sharp *speeding-up* of the pace of accumulation are being added others originating from the outside.

The new leadership of the Chinese Communist Party has been condemned by history. In the long run it can only suffer defeats, as the entire history of revisionism shows. It will therefore be forced increasingly to reveal its true face—which will become apparent to those who cannot or will not see this today. Actually, this leadership is sitting on a volcano. Even if it believes its own promises, these can only be refuted by facts. True, production may advance for a few years, especially in those branches of industry being given priority, but eventually the contradictions between industry and agriculture, town and country, mental work and manual work, accumulation and consumption, will worsen, for the road along which the present leadership of the party is leading China is the capitalist road.

It may be that the majority of the Chinese people believe that the party is still leading them along the socialist road, and that the promises made will be kept. This circumstance, together with the mistakes made by the Four, and weariness with their coercive measures, explains why a section of the masses has greeted the present leadership with relief and even, in some cases, with comparative enthusiasm.

However, things will change when the falsity of the promises made becomes clear. Then the Chinese people, who have waged long and victorious struggles for socialism, who have experienced the Cultural Revolution, who have seen in practice the positive political and economic results of this revolution, and who have learned to challenge the ruling authorities—this people so rich in experience will resume their forward march.

We cannot foresee when and how this will happen. In the meantime many zigzags may occur, including fresh splits in the party leadership, where a conflict appears to be growing between the classical revisionist line of Teng Hsiao-ping and the line of Hua Kuo-feng, who seems to want to preserve the outward forms of certain elements of the Cultural Revolution. But these fluctuations can only be secondary. It is the Chinese people who will decide, and they will have with them the sound elements in the Chinese Communist Party.

In the situation that exists today, China's friends abroad have the duty more than ever of standing by the Chinese people. Without interfering in China's affairs, they must avoid, above all, doing anything that might strengthen the prestige of the leaders who are dragging China along a road that leads to catastrophe. Furthermore, in face of the disillusionment of those in the rest of the world who see the Cultural Revolution being repudiated, without always understanding why, and who may come to despair of socialism, China's friends must try to explain how and why a revisionist line has momentarily triumphed. This explanation is all the more necessary because it can serve to reveal the roots of the mistakes made by the supporters of Mao Tse-tung's line, mistakes which resulted in their defeat. This knowledge is essential for all who want to fight for socialism, so as to limit the danger that these same mistakes may be reproduced in their own country or elsewhere.

This task of explanation is long and complex. I have tried to begin it in the last sections, but I am well aware that this is, at best, only a first step in a long process of reflection, in which many people will have to take part if it is to succeed. In any case, thank you, dear Neil Burton, for having, by your letter, stimulated me to reply and so to put into writing the few contributions toward an explanation which I have offered here.

Charles Bettelheim

Notes

1. I come back to this question later, in the sections on the Shanghai Commune.

2. As this letter is intended for publication I am giving, either in the text or in various notes, details regarding points which may not necessarily be known to, or remembered by, all my readers. Thus I shall remind them that the Four belonged to the highest reaches of the Chinese Communist Party. Wang Hung-wen was vice-chairman of the party beginning in August 1973. Chang Chun-chiao was a member of the standing committee of the Political Bureau. Yao Wen-yuan and Chiang Ching were members of the Political Bureau in 1969. They were arrested in October 1976, when Hua Kuo-feng carried out his *coup d'état*, and in July 1977 were all four expelled from the party "for life."

3. Karl Marx, Frederick Engels, and V.I. Lenin, *Anarchism and Anarcho-Syndicalism* (Moscow: Progress Publishers, 1972), p. 102.

4. Harry Braverman, *Labor and Monopoly Capital* (New York: Monthly Review Press, 1974), p. 16.

   Dealing with the discipline imposed on the workers in the capitalist factory, Marx writes that "this discipline will become superfluous under a social system in which the labourers work for their own account..." (*Capital*, Vol. III [Moscow: Foreign Languages Publishing House, 1959], p. 83).

5. See "About the General Program of Activity of the Party and the State," a document drawn up under the direction of Teng Hsiao-ping.

6. At the beginning of the 1970s "social profit" was often advocated. This meant that within certain limits the "financial losses" of some enterprises were tolerated, especially when these losses were connected with measures advantageous to the people—for example, in the form of the fight against pollution. By making it an unconditional requirement that every production unit must make a profit, in the financial sense, there was no longer any question of taking into account the various forms of "social profit" which might result from the working of this or that unit of production.

7. Karl Marx, *Capital*, vol. I (Harmondsworth: Penguin Books), pp. 697-8.

8. There are few estimates available of the volume of agricultural production, especially of the (decisive) production of "food-

grains,"̤ and these must be quoted with reservation. The latest production figure from a Chinese source, which was given to Western visitors, was, as far as I am aware, that for the harvest of 1974, given as 274.9 million tons. This was a record figure (it included tubers, and probably soya seeds as well; it is not known whether the tonnage of rice was calculated in terms of husked or unhusked rice). In 1975 foreign specialists, basing themselves mainly on statements made by provincial authorities, estimated the harvest at 280 or 290 million tons. Official announcements seem to indicate that the 1977 harvest reached that same level. These two years would have seen an increase corresponding, at best, to the increase in population. It remains true that between 1970 and 1975 the production of cereals increased by 47 million tons, or more than 19 percent—a remarkable achievement. We note, moreover, that China's contracts for imports of cereals amounted in 1977 to a record figure of 11 million tons, as against 5 million in 1975 and 2 million in 1976. (These figures are taken from *Le Monde* of January 10, 1977, *China Quarterly* of June 1976, pp. 817-21, and *Est-Ouest*, no. 4, 1977, p. 112.) For those who claim that the years 1965-77 were marked by an attitude of indifference toward production, it is not without point to recall that the total irrigated agricultural area of China increased from 35 million hectares in 1964 to about 55 million in 1977—an increase of some 20 million hectares (in 1952 the irrigated area came to 21 million hectares). (See Dwight H. Perkins, "Constraints Influencing China's Agriculture Performance," in *China: A Reassessment of the Economy* [Washington, D.C.: G.P.O., 1975], p. 28, and *Est-Ouest*, no. 4, 1977, p. 82.)

9. I consider later how these technological problems are presented predominantly in terms of the "mechanization of agriculture," and the social and political reasons why this is the case.

10. There are evidently contradictions, on this point as on others, within the leadership of the Chinese Communist Party. It is symptomatic that on December 25, 1977, New China News Agency (NCNA) circulated Mao Tse-tung's letter on agricultural mechanization, dated March 12, 1966, a letter which, while favoring such mechanization, warned against the illusions that may be cherished regarding the effects it can have, and against the tendency to want to go too fast in this direction. Mao Tse-tung noted in this letter that "it would be inadmissible to set to

work impulsively," and added: "Is not Soviet agriculture practically mechanized? Why, then, is it still in difficulties? This certainly calls for thought."

11. This "explanation" of the factory's attitude is disturbingly rem-
iniscent of the stereotyped replies given in the 1930s in the Soviet
Union to those who complained of the bad way the economy was
functioning: exhaustion of stocks, decline in the quality of products, etc. Everything was blamed on "Trotskyist sabotage," yet,
forty years after the "liquidation of the Trotskyists," the same
phenomena recur. Incidentally, it is worth noting that the
Hsiehtun commune contrasts the attitude of the Red East factory
to that of a sewing-machine factory which supplied the spare
parts asked for at once. Oddly enough, this was the No. 1
Sewing-Machine Factory in *Shanghai*—the place where the so-
called Gang of Four were alleged to be "rampant."

12. It will be noted how an incident like this provides an opportunity
for the cadres and technicians of the commune and the factory
to travel at the expense of their respective organs, that is, not to
work for several days, at the same time as heavy emphasis is
placed on the extra effort that the workers and peasants are expected to make. This throws light on the way class relations are
evolving.

13. The problem of spare parts is only one aspect of the contradictions engendered by a brusque speeding-up of agricultural
mechanization. These contradictions lead inevitably to a *gigan-
tic squandering* of machines, for the latter are sent into the
country districts before the conditions needed for their proper
use have been realized (the Chinese press is full of information on
this subject). Another problem is the maintenance of these
machines. It is not accidental that the editorial in *Jen-min Jih-
pao* of September 16, 1977, observes that the operators of
agricultural machinery who have been trained in the state
schools constitute only a small percentage of the total number
needed.

14. This conception accords greater importance to the accumulation
of equipment than to collective mastery of the production process by the producers.

15. The possibilities of increased output inherent in these methods
are considerable. It is their use, much more than mechanization,
that explains the high yields attained in other countries of Asia.
Thus in 1974 Japan's grain yield was 5,580 kg. per hectare, com-

pared with 1,900 kg. in China. For unhusked rice their respective yields were 6,200 kg. and 3,509 kg. (see *Est-Ouest*, no. 4,
1977, pp. 83-85).

16. I deal with this question in volume 3 of *Class Struggles in the
USSR*, which I am now writing.

17. I obviously have no room here to analyze in what way the present
revisionist line, whose principal representative is Teng Hsiao-
ping, resembles the revisionist line of the early 1960s, which Liu
Shao-chi and his supporters followed, and in what way it differs.
It seems to me that the principal difference lies in the emphasis
laid, today, on *accelerating* the pace of industrialization, on
"modernization," etc. The difference is connected, apparently,
with the numerical strengthening of the state bourgeoisie, which
is thus able to assert more strongly its hegemony over the old
bourgeoisie.

   This difference is also connected with the fact that, in order to
try and break the resistance, which can only grow, of a working
class which has experienced the Cultural Revolution, it is
necessary for the bourgeoisie to work up the myth of "urgency,"
of a "race against time." In the name of this "necessary struggle"
the state bourgeoisie tries to strengthen discipline to the utmost
and to increase the pace of work as much as possible. The wage
increases "granted" in 1977 thus appear both as a means of
dividing the working class (through the criteria governing these
increases) and as a necessary counterpart to tightening discipline
and raising the intensity of labor.

18. Recognizing these important contributions made by Chang must
not, of course, lead us to overlook the weak points in his analyses,
which indicate some of the limits which have objectively
restricted the development of Marxism in China. One of these
weak points is an inability to present the prospect of real *social
appropriation* through a revolutionary change in the production
relations. Instead of this prospect, what Chang advocated was
generalization of state ownership (mistakenly called "ownership
of the whole people"), whereas this would merely maintain the
separation of the immediate producers from their means of production. Similarly, Chang did not see that, as soon as state
ownership becomes predominant, the *principal* danger of
capitalist development lies in the development of bourgeois relations in the state sector, and no longer in petty commodity
production.

19. The figures quoted are given in "The Chinese Economy in 1976," *China Quarterly*, June 1977, pp. 362-4 and 382.
20. See USCIA, *People's Republic of China: Handbook of Economic Indicators*, August 1976, p. 1, quoted in *Est-Ouest*, no. 4, 1977, p. 97. According to this same source, tractor production (in thousand units of 15 h.p.) increased in this same period from 23.9 to 180, and that of merchant ships (in tons) from 50,600 to 335,600.
21. Figures from *China Quarterly*, June 1977, note 9.
22. *Peking Review*, no. 1, 1977, pp. 23-23. The version circulated by the Red Guards is in *Communism*, no. 1, November 1972, p. 95, and in Mao Tse-tung, *Textes 1949-1958* [Paris: Editions du Cerf, 1975], p. 190.
23. This observation seems to me especially important when dealing with the revolutionary line which was put into effect between 1966 and 1976. The actual political line of those years was strongly affected by the fact that the most consistent revolutionary leaders (which means, first and foremost, Mao himself) were relatively more isolated than for a long time had been supposed. They were able to make their views prevail only partially, because they were obliged to rely on social and political forces which were extremely diverse and which differed from one period to another. For example, they relied upon radicalized elements of the petty bourgeoisie in the first months of the Cultural Revolution, then upon a section of the People's Liberation Army, and so on. (On this point, see also my remarks below on the Shanghai Commune, and especially note 53.)
24. See *Peking Review*, no. 41, 1976, p. 5. See also the chronology of the events of this period given in A. Bouc, *La Rectification* (Paris, 1977), pp. 159 ff., and Chen Ying-hsiang and Claude Cadart, *Les Deux Morts de Mao Tsé-toung* (Paris, 1977), pp. 97 ff. These two books present views which differ widely from mine, as well as from each other.
25. See Chen Ying-hsiang and Claude Cadart, *Les Deux Morts*, p. 98.
26. At best, a section of the standing committee of the Political Bureau may have met.
27. As K.S. Karol notes in his contribution, entitled "Da Teng a Teng: Tre anni di lotta politica in Cina," in *Quale Cina dopo la revoluzione culturale, Il Manifesto*, no. 6, p. 46.
28. See *Peking Review*, nos. 43 and 44, 1976.

29. On October 29 *Chiehfangchun Bao* published an article entitled "Comrade Hua Kuo-feng is Undeniably the Leader of Our Party." Such an assertion doubtless implied that the fact was not obvious to everyone.

30. Besides, if this campaign were not made up of lies, what sort of a party would it be whose leaders had done all that is alleged against the Four, without anybody ever knowing or protesting?

31. In Hua's speech of November 24, when the first stone of Mao Tse-tung's mausoleum was laid, there was no more criticism of Teng.

32. Some of these executions were announced officially, either over the radio or by means of posters displayed by the authorities. Others became known through "big-character posters" or because people saw trucks carrying persons condemned to death, wearing placards around their necks which proclaimed the sentence passed upon them. Matters went so far that it became necessary to state officially that it might be desirable to suspend certain executions. It is hard to say with certainty that the executions carried out during the struggle against the Rightists were less numerous than these. Despite what is being said now, however, this would appear to have been the case. The present comeback of the Rightists to positions of leadership shows, in any event, that *they* had merely been removed from their responsibilities. Besides, Mao Tse-tung's line was opposed to large-scale execution of counter-revolutionaries. Thus, in *On the Ten Major Relationships*, Mao wrote: "What harm is there in not killing any of them? Those who are physically fit for manual labor should be reformed through labor ... You can make them perform some kind of service to the people ... Second, people may be wrongly executed. Once a head is chopped off, history shows it cannot be restored, nor can it grow again as chives do, after being cut. If you cut off a head by mistake, there is no way to rectify the mistake, even if you want to.... Adopting the policy of killing none when eliminating counter-revolutionaries from party and government organs in no way prevents us from being strict with them." (*Peking Review*, no. 1, 1977. See also Mao Tse-tung, *Textes 1949-1958*, p. 186).

33. For instance, Hu Yao-pang became head of this department in December 1977. Formerly secretary-general of the Young Communist League, he was severely criticized during the Cultural Revolution for his revisionist conceptions.

34. See the article by Alain Jacob in *Le Monde*, January 13, 1978.
35. Is it necessary to recall that when Hua Kuo-feng was appointed acting deputy prime minister in February 1976, he proposed that the campaign to criticize Teng Hsiao-ping be launched under the party's leadership? This fact was mentioned by the army daily on November 8, 1976, but Hua obviously said nothing further about it at the Eleventh Congress (see *Quale Cina*, pp. 42-43).
36. W. Aschmoneit develops this line of thought in his article "China: Die Privilegierung der Intelligenz," *Berliner Hefte*, January 1978, pp. 27 ff.
37. As Aschmoneit rightly asks, what do we know about this differentiation beyond the fact that eight grades of wages exist? What do we know about differences in skill, about the role of seasonal workers, about relations between the workers in the small and medium factories of the country areas and the workers in the big factories in the towns? (ibid., p. 32).
38. Aschmoneit notes also that we know practically nothing about the effects on social differentiation in the countryside of the campaigns to change the production processes which followed the establishment of the people's communes.
39. And even at the time the communes were founded, these terms referred, in general, to social differentiation prior to the land reform, which is more than twenty-five years behind us.
40. When former cadres removed from office for having acted in an "incorrect" way are denounced, the recourse to *stereotypes* is also normal. They are almost all accused of being "spies" or "secret agents." It was in these terms that Chiang Ching attacked a number of writers and artists during the Cultural Revolution, and it is in these terms that she is now being attacked in turn. Here, too, "labels" are being "stuck on," instead of a concrete analysis being made. The repetition of this method implies that, instead of matters being explained to the masses, they are being refused any explanation. In this way their own history is *obscured*, and an attempt is made to *destroy their historical memory*, and so to *disarm* them, by the use of mutilated or forged documents and falsified photographs. When that happens, it is no longer a question of mere lack of analysis but of contempt for the masses.
41. This forward thrust developed from the summer of 1966 onward. It was preceded by an intense ideological class struggle in

which the students and young workers played the role of a *vanguard*. During my visits to factories in the summer of 1967, the members of the revolutionary factory committees explained to me more than once that, at the beginning of the Cultural Revolution, most of the workers did not feel directly concerned, and often even sent away the students and young workers from other factories who wanted to talk with them. It was only little by little, through intense propaganda efforts, that the broad masses of the workers were brought into movement. I drew the attention of Maria Antonietta Macciocchi to this dialectic. She has retained from what I said to her the idea that in my view the Cultural Revolution was not a genuine mass movement but "the ideological attempt of a vanguard to impose its own line and, as a result, the birth of a new, antibureaucratic bureaucracy" (M.A. Macciocchi, *Après Marx, Avril* [Paris: Editions de Seuil, 1978], pp. 26-27). It is clear that a vanguard which had tried to "impose" itself would never have succeeded in unleashing such a mass movement as was the Cultural Revolution.

42. To discover the reasons for this inability would require prolonged and complex analyses which I cannot undertake here, and for which, moreover, I lack the materials. These reasons were, certainly, at once social, ideological and political. I shall mention some of them later. From the ideological standpoint these reasons were connected with the very insufficient break those concerned had made with the anti-Marxist conceptions of the Stalin epoch.

43. Aschmoneit, "China," p. 30

44. Coercion did not necessarily or even frequently take the form of coercion by "administrative means," but rather of "social pressure." Further, it must be remembered that the problem of the departure (voluntary in varying degrees) of young people to the country districts affected not only the children of intellectuals but also those of workers.

45. In the last part of the second volume of *Class Struggles in the USSR* (New York: Monthly Review Press, 1978) I have analyzed the process of transformation undergone by Bolshevik ideology. There is no room to go over this again here.

46. See Aschmoneit's remarks on this subject, "China," p. 31.

47. This document, dated November 17, 1966, was published by the newspaper of the Red Guards of the Peking Aeronautical Institute on December 23 (see Chinese Communist Party,

Documents of the Great Cultural Proletarian Revolution [Hongkong: URI, 1966], p. 133).

48. An account of these events is given in K.S. Karol, *The Second Chinese Revolution* (London: Jonathan Cape, 1975), pp. 215 ff.
49. *Peking Review*, January 26, 1967, pp. 8-9.
50. Editorial of February 6, 1967, in *Wen Hui-pao*, the principal Shanghai newspaper, quoted in Karol, *The Second Chinese Revolution*, p. 227.
51. See ibid., pp. 229-31. Extensive extracts from this speech were reproduced in *Survey of the China Mainland Press*, no. 4147. See also Mao Tse-tung, *Le Grand Livre Rouge (1949-1971)* (Paris: Flammarion, 1975), pp. 224 ff.
52. See Jean Daubier, *Histoire de la Révolution Culturelle Prolétarienne en Chine (1965-1969)* (Paris: Maspero, 1970), pp. 289 ff.
53. As we know, the most consistent promoters of the revolutionary line were constantly obliged to rely upon (and to make compromises with) ideological and political trends of different kinds, owing to their minority position, which they proved unable to overcome. Thus, in his letter of July 8, 1966, to Chiang Ching, Mao said that, given the situation that existed, he could not avoid relying upon Lin Piao (and, therefore, upon the People's Liberation Army), even though he disagreed with him on some important points. As he wrote: "My friend [an ironical reference to Lin Piao] and his supporters have forced my hand. Apparently I am unable to do otherwise than agree with them." He even added: "This is the first time in my life that, on an essential problem, I find myself aligned with other people against my will. This is what is called changing one's direction without wanting to" (quoted in *Le Monde*, December 2, 1972). This comparative isolation of the revolutionary leaders had not been overcome by the time of the Ninth Party Congress in 1969. In 1971, with the fall of Lin Piao, this caused the revolutionary leaders to enter into agreement with civilian cadres who were far from sympathetic to the Cultural Revolution. These cadres constituted the social and political basis on which Hua Kuo-feng was to rely in his *coup d'état*.

I attempt later on to analyze some of the ideological reasons for this comparative isolation of the most consistent and most respected of the leaders advocating the revolutionary line; as for the *social basis* of this situation, that was doubtless constituted by the slight relative weight of the *Chinese proletariat*. The active elements of this class, especially among the young workers, formed a fundamental base upon which the revolutionary line's advocates were able to rely (and this was so to the very end), but it was a numerically weak base, so that various forms of agreement with petty-bourgeois trends had to be entered into. The need for these agreements, and the conditions under which they were concluded, hindered to some extent the development of more radical theoretical positions.

54. Quoted in Karol, *The Second Chinese Revolution*, pp. 218-19.
55. Ibid., p. 225.
56. In fact, the leaders of the People's Liberation Army played a decisive political role for several years. Some commanders were undoubtedly in favor of revolutionary positions and did really help the Left, but they were not the majority. The PLA was one of the apparatuses which had been least revolutionized. Between 1960 and 1965 it had, to be sure, experienced a movement for the study of Marxism, but this was conducted in the way in which Lin Piao conceived such a movement, a schematic and stereotyped way, so that, ultimately, it proved to be negative rather than positive in its effects. The relation of forces was never such as to enable the advocates of the revolutionary line really to tackle the problem of revolutionizing the PLA. In 1967 Mao was still hoping that the PLA would educate itself through its intervention in the Cultural Revolution (see J. Daubier, *Histoire*, p. 293). Facts have shown that this did not happen. The high command of the PLA eventually gave its support to the revisionist line. Furthermore, the effort put in by the Left to develop the workers' militias was not sufficiently sustained. Today these militias have been practically disarmed and put under the control of the PLA. At the same time, we see reappearing the anti-Marxist formulation which presents the PLA as "the pillar of the dictatorship of the proletariat."
57. Lenin, "Report on the Party Programme," Eighth Congress of the Russian Communist Party, March 19, 1919.
58. After the abandonment of the political form of the Shanghai Commune, tension between the role assigned to the party and that assigned to the masses recurred several times, but without resulting in any change in actual relations (for the same reasons as in 1967). Thus, in 1974 many Chinese workers raised this slogan: "We want to be masters of the state and of the factories,

not slaves of production and work." At that time they supported the advocates of the revolutionary line. Today, since the *coup d'état*, this slogan is regarded as "reactionary" (see P. Tissier, "La ligne économique de la nouvelle direction chinoise pendant l'anneé 1977," *Communisme*, November 1977-February 1978, pp. 68 ff.).

59. I have no room to deal with this important problem. Briefly, the weakness of these analyses is due to the fact that the Chinese Communist Party did not question the anti-Marxist conceptions developed by the Bolshevik Party during the 1930s. According to these conceptions, state ownership and collective-farm ownership are two forms of "socialist ownership." This idea is quite unsound. It does not relate to any change in production relations. Again, according to the conceptions developed by the Bolshevik Party during the 1930s, the revolution was supposed to have ensured the existence of a ruling authority based fundamentally on "proletarian political relations," which obscured the existence of a state machine separated from the masses and therefore reproducing bourgeois political relations. Consequently, if these conceptions are not subjected to criticism, one *cannot* indicate to the mass movement the *real targets* that it should set itself. On this question see B. Fabrègues, "Questions sur la théorie du socialisme," *Communisme*, November 1977-February 1978, pp. 40 ff. especially pp. 45-49.

60. The existence of these privileges can be clearly seen in Roxane Witke's biography of Chang Ching (*Comrade Chiang Ch'ing* [Boston: Little, Brown, 1977]). These were not privileges peculiar to a particular individual. All leaders of the same rank enjoyed them, although today the new leadership is trying to make out that only the Four possessed them. It is known that this is far from being the case, and that Teng Hsiao-ping does not hesitate to have friends of his with whom he wants to play bridge brought to Peking by airplane.

61. It is significant that in the discussions organized in the various "units" (factories, workshops, educational institutions, etc.) on "restriction of bourgeois right" and the application of the principle of "to each according to his work," what has mainly been dealt with is the problem of the eight-grade wage system, bonuses, and so on, whereas the matter of the high salaries of the state officials (who may receive more than ten times as much as a worker entering industry) does not seem, from the information

available, ever to have been debated, even in the years when discussions were at their "widest ranging."

62. On this point, see Bettelheim, *Class Struggles in the USSR: First Period, 1917-1923*, pp. 399 ff.

63. Generally speaking, restrictions on freedom of expression, information, and discussion (in the party and in the society as a whole), conceived as a means of "protecting" the revolutionary character of the ruling authority, very easily become transformed into their opposite. They make possible not merely the formation of cliques and the development of corruption and nepotism but also, what is even more serious, they favour the seizure of power by the state bourgeoisie. A *coup d'état* carried out by the latter enables them to exploit with ease the restrictions imposed on democracy so as to repress the revolutionaries. Today the experience of China, following that of the USSR, leaves room for no doubt on this score.

64. On the transformation of the Bolshevik ideological formation see *Class Struggles in the USSR: Second Period, 1924-1930* (New York: Monthly Review Press, 1978), chap. 1.

65. This idea was expressed clearly in 1964 in *On Khrushchev's Phoney Communism and Its Historical Lessons for the World*, (Peking: Foreign Languages Press, 1964), p. 72.

66. In *On the Correct Handling of Contradictions Among the People* (1957) Mao Tse-tung pointed out that it is useless to "ban the expression of wrong ideas," for "the ideas will still be there," and that "Marxism can only develop through struggle." In the same work he said that "a party as much as an individual has great need to hear opinions different from its own" and that "mutual supervision among the various parties" is necessary — that "the other democratic parties should exercise supervision over the Communist Party" (Mao Tse-tung, *On New Democracy* [Peking: Foreign Languages Press, 1967], pp. 151-58).

67. Such hindrances also stand in the way of what Marx calls "free scientific inquiry," which, he says, has many enemies (preface to the first edition of *Capital*).

68. These "hundred flowers" are evidently a mere façade, aimed in the main at deceiving the intellectuals, who have been granted a few minor "concessions." In part, these "concessions" correspond to the requirements for scientific and technological development which the revisionist line counts on achieving, but they can only

be limited in character. They conflict with the respect for authority and hierarchy which is constantly called for by the supporters of the revisionist line. Above all, these "liberal concessions" cannot develop, for they are not reconcilable with the repressions which the advocates of the revisionist line are being led to exert against the working people and against those cadres who are unwilling to repudiate their past. Thus *Jen-min Jih-pao* of February 13, 1978, called for all cadres who fail to take up "a firm position in the fight against the Gang of Four" to be attacked, so as to oblige them "to make a self-criticism and plainly confess their mistakes." The paper thereby revealed its fear lest these cadres become "inevitably" what it called "fomenters of [political] upheavals when a favorable situation presents itself" (quoted in *Le Monde*, February 17, 1978).

69. Thus, on December 27, 1977, there was held, for the first time for many years, an enlarged meeting of the standing committee of the Fourth National Conference of the Chinese People's Political Consultative Committee, a meeting in which the "democratic parties" took part (*Peking Review*, no. 1, 1978, p. 3).

70. What I am questioning here is the "Three Worlds Theory" itself. To start a discussion about this would take up too much space. Nevertheless, it must be said that this "theory" has no scientific basis. It corresponds to no reality. It wrongly assumes that, as between the "Second" and the "Third" worlds, unity can have primacy over contradiction, an idea which runs counter to everything taught us by history, past and present. History reveals the deep conflicts which set many of the countries of the "Second" and "Third" worlds against each other (as well as the acute conflicts between some of the countries of the "Third" world itself). History and present reality show us, too, how great are the relations of dependence binding most of the governments of these "worlds" to one or the other of the two superpowers. As I have said already, the "argument from authority" of those who claim that this theory derives from Mao Tse-tung cannot confer scientific value upon a theory which buries the class contradictions involved, to say nothing of the contradictions between countries. Besides which, even this claim does not seem to be well founded, since there is no published work of Mao's dealing with the matter. The first official proclamation of this "theory" occurred in Teng Hsiao-ping's speech at the United Nations.

71. On October 21, 1977, the ambassador of the People's Republic

of China to Chile declared that his impression of Chile and *"of its head of state, is excellent"* (*El Mercurio*, October 21, 1977, and *La Tercera* of the same day).

72. China is thus gradually losing the position it held as an example of a country capable of developing by means of its own resources.